THE GENIUS
IS INSIDE

Michel David

THE GENIUS IS INSIDE

A high performance step by step strategy development guide for small and medium size companies.

iUniverse, Inc.
Bloomington

iUniverse books may be ordered through booksellers or by contacting:

iUniverse
1663 Liberty Drive
Bloomington, IN 47403
www.iuniverse.com
1-800-Authors (1-800-288-4677)

ISBN: 978-1-4502-6881-3 (sc)
ISBN: 978-1-4502-6882-0 (ebook)

Library of Congress Control Number: 2010916061

Printed in the United States of America

iUniverse rev. date: 12/06/2010

To Rae
and my daughters

Contents

Preface:
The Problem We Want to Solve

The problem is as follows: strategy is an important driver of company success. But the processes that have been developed to create strategies were designed for large corporations, and even there, they are often ineffective. This is even more so for small and mid-sized companies.

This is a book about strategy formulation in small and mid-sized companies. These companies are critically important to the general economy: they create the majority of new jobs and most of the innovative ideas.

Being of smaller size, their growth potential is usually far greater. They are closer to their entrepreneurial origins and are thus most likely to adopt new breakthrough strategies to create a completely new growth curve. They still have one or more futures to create.

In order to fully exploit this potential they need frameworks, approaches and tools designed for their specific situation and challenges in critical areas such as strategy, business models, processes, people and disciplines.

Yet most of what is available to them has been designed for large corporations whose challenges in the main, deal with the optimization of the fruits of past successes.

Business strategy is a relatively new concept. It is over the past 50 years that the concept of strategy has come to dominate the thinking within the corporate world. This is the conclusion of Walter Kiechel III in his recent book, The Lords of Strategy. According to Mr. Kiechel, strategy has contributed to the renewal of competitive strength in many companies and industries which would otherwise have fallen by the wayside. The main trust of these developments has been optimization, or Greater Taylorism as he calls it!

The development and growth of business strategy has been driven by consultants and academics. The three larger strategy firms: Bain, the Boston Consulting Group and McKinsey have been the main drivers of this evolution. Thus the principal marketplace for strategy has been large corporations serviced by large consulting firms.

This is fine as far as it goes. But what about small and mid-sized firms? The strategic planning processes that have been developed by the large firms for their large clients have significant drawbacks for mid-tier companies:

- They involve heavy analytical efforts, usually done by the consultants. This is an approach that small and medium-sized companies simply cannot afford.
- Because the clients are larger, established organizations, the planning frameworks tend to be **defensive**. The main question for them is "how do we protect and optimize what we have?"

The challenge of small and medium-sized firms is quite different. They are the attackers rather than the defenders; they are at the base or mid way up, but surely not at the top of the mountain. We would propose that their main issues are related to **growth** as opposed to optimization. They need to win to-day, just like the larger corporations, but most important they have to create the next growth curve in order to exploit their full potential.

For small and mid-sized companies, many of the concepts that are prevalent in the main strategy marketplace (large corporations/ large consulting firms) are of little value and possibly dysfunctional. For example, Henry Mintzberg recently argued that *shareholder value* as a holy grail has focused senior management attention on *productivity gains*. The strategy has been to *downsize* and *cut costs*. The consequent thinning out of middle management has resulted in loss of knowledge, creativity, community, trust, and commitment. Having let go of their knowledge, companies must resort to superstar CEOs (with supersize compensation) to "shake things up." This only compounds the vicious circle of increased cynicism, loss of trust, and decreased collaboration.

Our purpose in this book is to put all such noise aside and start from the needs that are specific to the mid-tier marketplace. This requires a framework and a process that is designed from the ground up.

This is a situation similar to what the Detroit Big 3 had to face when the first oil crisis created demand for small or smaller cars. The Big 3 tried to shrink down their large models. Remember the Cadillac Cimaron? The Europeans and the Japanese, for reasons specific to their own national markets, had small cars designed from the ground up to be small cars. Remember the Beetle, the Honda Civic, the Toyota Corolla?

To our knowledge, this has not yet been done in the strategy domain. This is the problem we want to solve. To propose a process of strategy formulation that addresses the specific needs of mid-tier companies, namely:

- **Strategy** frameworks that include the prevalent positioning concepts but add intent and radical innovation, the attacker's edge.
- **Business models**, "how we work together" based on collaboration rather than command-and-control hierarchies.
- **Processes** designed for simplicity and speed and that minimize the conditions for power and politics to take hold. This should be the normal condition in smaller organizations but they will be subjected to the same pressures as older established organizations as they grow themselves.
- **People** policies and practices that create high commitment and ownership by all as opposed to the traditional contractual approach which leads to the "Us and Them" opposition.
- **Discipline** for the follow-up that is necessary for anything to happen. The methodologies for discipline that are proposed in this book apply equally to large and small organizations, the differentiator in both cases is the management leadership required to make things happen.

This book is written from the perspective of strategy and the strategic planning process but it aims to propose a complete enterprise system for mid-tier companies.

This book also aims to provide a **template for high-performance business firms** that are world-class or aiming to be the best in the world. If they are asked, everyone will say they want to do that. But of course, few actually walk the talk.

So our goal is to provide an effective process and a complete enterprise model for an excellence-driven audience of mid-tier business firms.

Given that the author's work experience has been mostly in North America, the ideas and the examples in the book are anchored in that culture. And even in North America, only a minority of companies operate and provide the models that are used in this book. But they exist, and we sorely need more of them. The application of these models in cultures other than North America would require integration with these cultures, one by one, respecting the specificity of each.

The book will follow the logic of the consulting approach we propose for companies to formulate the strategy that will create their future. First, agree on your current state, then design your target state. Getting from here to there typically involves three types of strategies: alignment, incremental innovation, and radical innovation. Each of these three strategies has its specific logic and methodologies. Ideally, they are pursued one after the other to avoid overloading the process and not succeeding at any. This can be illustrated as follows:

The Book in One Picture

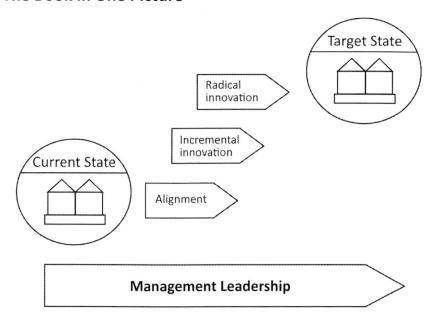

More specifically, the chapters of the book deal with the following materials:

- Chapter 1 starts with the mission of the strategic planning process: to **Create the Future**. The planning process should provide the frameworks and the tools to do this.
- The starting point is to recognize that each situation is unique, and therefore that no two strategies are alike. The process starts with a full and candid **assessment** of the current position and prospects. The aim is to produce an agreed definition of the current business model. This is chapter 2.
- The next question deals with the required **target model** to create the next growth curve. The right organization and the right players have the best chance of getting to the right strategy. This is chapter 3.
- The first level of strategy is **alignment** in and around the current business model. Viewed through the lenses of **high-performance management**, and when combined with incremental innovation, there is almost no limit to the growth and performance potential of the current business model. This is chapter 4.
- **Incremental innovation** applies to the current business model. In this sense, chapter 5 is a continuation of chapter 4. But innovation requires its own specific process, and this is the object of chapter 5.
- **Radical innovation** causes significant and recognized change to a given domain. This process finds new spaces, and it imposes new rules. Radical innovation comes from sources and processes that are different from incremental innovation. But incremental innovation creates the fertile ground for radical innovation. This is chapter 6.
- Finally, nothing happens without follow-up, and change requires management. This is the **leader's work**, and it starts by working on one's self. This is chapter 7.

Chapter 1: Strategic Planning Creates the Future

It is at the moments of commencements that we need to balance the equilibriums precisely.
—Ancient wisdom

1.1   What is Strategy?

Until recently, the concept of strategy was applied to the fields of political and military affairs. It is only in the last fifty years or so that strategy was introduced and has come to dominate the thinking within the corporate world. Yet, there is no commonly agreed definition.

In the fields of politics and military affairs, strategy can be used at different levels such as national or grand strategy, then to a specific theater or within that, at the operational, tactical and technical levels. But according to Edward N. Lutvak "…Our subject is as varied as human life, often charged with powerful emotions, constrained by institutional habits and urges…so that definitional nets made by abstract phrasemaking can capture only the hollow forms of strategy and not its protean content" (p. 71).

The object of political and military strategy is power. The stakes for business strategy are economic, be it market share or shareholder value. The object is different and so are the analytical methods and the results.

In the field of business, strategy has been defined from at least three different perspectives: positioning and differentiation, insight and finally intent.

For Michael Porter strategy is a series of choices about **targeting**, **positioning** and **differentiation**. It is as much about "what to do" as about "what not to do". Such a perspective has proven most useful, especially in sharpening competitive performance at the business unit level. But this framework tends to keep strategic thinking at the level of "more and better of the same". There is a lot of value there, but not much attention is paid to the creation of new breakthrough strategies.

Andrew Campbell has tried to take the strategy framework one step further by defining it as a unique insight about how to create more value than competitors.

Gary Hamel and C.K. Prahalad have presented a point of view that starts from the destination point rather than the departure point. Their question is "what do we want to be?", i.e. what is our strategic intent rather than "more and better of the same".

Walter Kiechel III, previously cited in the preface, has surveyed the field of strategy over the past fifty years. He concludes that most of the conceptual framework of most of the applications of strategy in the business area has been focused on "more and better of the same", on optimization of economic results. Such an approach is an adaptation and an answer to what he calls the "fierce capitalism" that results from globalization and the ever increasing appetite of investors for ever greater returns. This is most likely to continue.

This leaves some major unanswered questions for current strategy frameworks: is there another superordinate goal to be proposed instead of maximization of shareholder value? How are the ever widening income gaps between senior managers and workers to be addressed? And from a North American perspective, is there an organization model that can take our companies to a renewed competitive edge, to a "next curve".

A recent IBM Global CEO study found that financial outperformers are making bolder plays. These companies anticipate more change and manage it better. They are also more global in their business designs, partner more extensively, and choose more disruptive forms of business model innovation.

Kiechel thinks there are some models that provide useful ideas. He proposes the large strategy consulting firms as examples. They have a more integrative approach which includes people's individual aspirations and a very strong client focus. Their practices stress hiring decisions, performance evaluation after every project, junior staff evaluating senior staff, counseling out those who will not reach the higher levels, multidimensional evaluations of partners by partners and elected leaders for fixed terms. They are meritocratic systems that create a sense of fairness and support for entrepreneurial risk taking.

This book is positioned to this emerging point of view and how it applies to mid-tier companies. Our goal is to present an integrative framework where shareholder value is the result, not the goal, of doing very well by your clients and your people. This by winning today and creating a successful future.

1.2   The Challenge of the Second Curve

Organizations are living organisms, and as such, they eventually die. It is only a question of when. The **life cycle curve**, sometimes called the "S" curve, is a useful way to discuss a company's current position and its consequent strategic challenge. This curve was originally used in technological innovation to explain the sometimes very long periods before a new technology is adopted. For example, it took fifty years for television to become a commercial success. Then, when general adoption occurs, growth can be explosive. Eventually, growth markets become replacement markets. This curve is also used in marketing to explain the patterns of adoption of new products or concepts by opinion leaders.

Business strategies also follow an "S" curve pattern. Finding a creative insight and an entrepreneurial leader, financing its roll out, and orchestrating its successful expansion can take a long time. The growth phase usually involves better-than-average results, and at maturity the battle is for market share and relative cost efficiency. Eventually, decline occurs. When this is not addressed properly, the company disappears.

This is a problem and also a great opportunity for established companies or for their challengers. The outcome depends on who will invent the second, and eventually, the third curve.

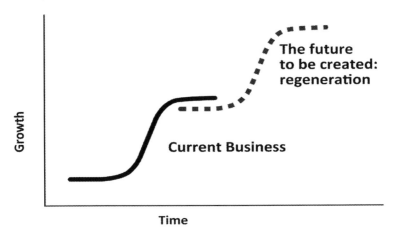

Figure 1.1. Where is our future?

1.3 The Future Is Open

Today's actions have consequences. These consequences are not linear or predetermined. A specific action could have two, three, or four different consequences. Some of these consequences have varying degrees of probability that they will happen. Some are very high, while others are very low.

Possibilities become reality when someone bets on them. There is no guarantee of success for either high- or low-probability events. But it is most likely that those who do not place any bets at all will end up in an unremarkable position.

Those who decide to place bets, to create and be part of the future, need to have a game plan. Most simply, they can rely on **luck**. Things happen, and opportunities arise. People who are open to the future and who are willing to place bets will act on some or most of these opportunities. Some bets may very well be successful, and a second curve is then created.

But luck only goes so far, and companies should not rely on luck alone. They should be proactive in creating their future. They must establish a systematic approach, where learning is based on **trial and error**. Both successes and failures create new knowledge that can serve as the next platform for new initiatives.

This process, to sustain a better present and to create the future, needs to be driven by a framework that defines principles and assumptions about target states, the sources of possibilities, the procedure of trial and opportunity selection, and how to make initiatives happen. This process and the organization to execute it successfully is what we will address in this book.

1.4   The Value Created by Strategic Planning

Strategy consists of the choices a company makes about its goals, its philosophy, its domain of activity, its competitive environment, and the actions that will take it from its current state to its target state.

Strategic planning is a process that sometimes produces strategy and at other times fails utterly to produce any strategy. At a minimum, strategic planning processes provide analysis of markets, competition, current position, and performance: strengths, weaknesses, opportunities, and threats. Many stop there and do not address the "so what?" question—and even less the "what is the opportunity?" question. They fail to examine the implications of whatever facts have been discovered.

Some have argued that strategic planning should limit itself to analysis and assume that strategic insight comes from a creativity that needs to happen, or can only happen, outside the constraints of such a formal analytical process.

Another way to look at it is to design the planning process so that it provides a venue for creative insight and breakthrough strategies. Such a process is different from the purely analytical approach by its framework, its methodologies, and the people who are called upon to participate. This book is dedicated to this approach, which can be defined around three main questions:

> **"Where are we?"**
> **"Who are we?"**
> **"What will we do?"**

Answering these questions over time with discipline and creativity creates a company's future.

5

I. "Where Are We?"

A fact-based, insightful assessment of the current situation is the foundation of any valid strategy formulation. This is the subject of the next chapter. At this point in the discussion, what is required is an understanding of the context in which strategic planning will take place.

Most strategic planning happens in what consulting engineers call "brownfield" situations, in other words, situations that already exist, that have a legacy. This is what most of us have to deal with most of the time.

A few such "brownfield" companies are already leaders in their domain. They **dominate** their current competitive arena. Most, however, find themselves in the middle or at the bottom of the pyramid; they are currently **followers**.

Sometimes, not very often, new "greenfield" situations happen. Here, the designers can implement directly from their model or target state "Haussmann's plan d'urbanisme." This is a once-in-a-lifetime opportunity to start at the state of the art, both technologically and managerially. The challenge here is to design well.

Of course, after they start operating, greenfield situations become brownfield and the full logic of the strategic planning process is required, including an assessment of the current situation.

II. "Who Are We?"

Busy results-driven executives may become quickly impatient with discussions of models or target states. Nevertheless, this is a fundamental element of the strategy process, because it is what guides which choices to make, which initiatives "fit," and which do not.

A model of the enterprise, what Peter Drucker calls a "theory of the business" (*Innovation and entrepreneurship*, New York: Harper & Row, 1985) defines the business; for instance:

- Its domain of activity and the dynamics within that domain
- Its goal

6

- Its core competencies
- Its rules of the game, its non-negotiables

The strategic planning process should produce a statement defining the current model, the **current state**. It may also, depending on the level of change that will result from a new strategy, produce a future model, the **target state**.

This is not an easy, straightforward affair. Models are often hard to define, they will evolve through time, and they cannot be produced by analytics only. Models come from the leaders and their vision of the company.

III. "What Will We Do?"

Defining what we will do is a disciplined three-level **process**.

It is not made any easier by the fact that there is no generally accepted definition of strategy in general and business strategy in particular. But there are ways to think about the **strategic problem**, the challenge of the second curve, namely **winning today**, and most importantly **how to create the future**.

The first view of strategy is to build from what you have to what you would like to have. The key question is "what are our options given our current assets and position?" This **strategic positioning** view is particularly useful to address the winning-today part of the strategic problem. Michael Porter has developed this approach particularly well.

The second point of view is to start from an intention: "What do we want to become?" This discussion may actually not be related to the current position or level of assets. It can be a twenty-five-year goal that a company can pursue through many shorter-term strategic cycles, and not necessarily in a perfectly straight line. Gary Hamel and C. K. Prahalad have made the case for this "strategic intent" view of business strategy.

These two points of view do not require a forced choice. They are both necessary to completely answer the full today/tomorrow strategic problem.

So how does one get the benefit of both views? In our experience, by pursuing three levels of strategy formulation, as follows:

- **Alignment** deals with the current business. Its focus is on performance: competitive, operational, and managerial.
- **Incremental innovation** aims to create new value in and around the current business model.
- **Radical innovation** takes nothing for granted; its domain is new spaces and new rules.

Each of these levels of strategy requires specific methodologies. They will be described in later chapters. In their application, we have found that it is next to impossible to address all three at the same time. This usually creates overload and inhibits creativity, and the unfortunate result is that nothing gets done very well. It is more productive to add the next level of planning incrementally through subsequent cycles.

At each level, the quality of the output will increase if participation in the process is wider rather than narrower and if care is taken to include new, different voices in the choice of participants.

It is this disciplined three-level process that produces the target model. Actually, it is an evolving target model, a prototype that improves at each step and through ongoing strategic decision-making.

1.5 Pitfalls to Avoid in the Planning Process

Strategic planning is the business process that companies can use to create their future. Strategic planning can take many forms. It can consist of pure entrepreneurial insight to highly formalized processes. But in one way or another, a company will work towards a rich and superior future if strategic planning has a clear, overarching goal of adding value. Such value is added by defining how to create a winning future, just as other business processes contribute in their way to the company's overall management system. For example:

- Being the employer of choice is the end goal for human resources processes.

- Superior quality and cost competitiveness is the goal for Continuous-improvement processes.
- Best information, produced just in time, is the goal for information technology processes.

For many companies, strategic planning does not contribute, or it contributes only marginally, to the creation of the future. Much effort is expanded for little value added. This situation has been surveyed extensively. The most frequent causes of this value gap are as follows:

- The process is too focused on analysis. This is the paralysis by analysis syndrome.
- The process becomes bureaucratic, there is hardly any strategic or entrepreneurial input.
- The process has not clearly been assigned the goal of creating the future.

Yet, strategic planning is a mature methodology that has been used extensively for the past fifty years. Its value-adding challenge is not to find analytical breakthroughs, although such innovations always add to the process. The main question should be about the goals, alignment, and a pipeline of new business initiatives. Methodologies can always be aligned effectively to produce agreed targets.

1.6   Management: The Good, the Bad, and the Ugly

Excellent strategic planning that produces a winning strategy does not happen in a vacuum. Strategy is senior management's responsibility. It will most likely be outstanding in an environment that applies high-quality management practices:

- A clear code applied with integrity
- Coherent, mutually reinforcing management systems
- High-performance business processes and work design
- Disciplined execution and follow-up: balanced priorities, realistic critical path

Most companies do not meet this test; some by a little, others by a lot.

The mildly dysfunctional are often characterized by "busyness." This is the "We don't have the time" problem. People work hard, but everything is equally important. From a strategy-process perspective, the analytics are poor or simply not done, and there is little if any space to produce creative insight.

At the worst, in the "ugly" situations, management throws away its opportunity. This is the "false start" problem. In such situations, the design of a clear target state would have provided the decision framework to avoid dissipation of precious resources and an effective roadmap to exploit the opportunity at hand. Instead, all efforts get concentrated on a few immediate, "burning" projects; meanwhile, low-fit decisions are taken elsewhere. Foundations are laid in cement before the building is designed.

The strategy process should be participative. However, strategy is senior management's responsibility: it starts there, and it ends there.

Chapter 2: Each Situation Is Unique

Knowing oneself is the start of wisdom, therefore of regeneration.
—Krishnamurti, *The First and Last Freedom*

2.1 Situation Analysis: The "Where Are We?" Question

Each company and each business unit within a company is unique because of its mandate, products, technologies, competitive set, history, and people.

Why is it necessary to make an assessment? Because one must understand the organization's present and its past. The present is not the future, but it is essential to understand it insightfully and truthfully in order to start building the future. We always assume we have a good grasp of the current situation. Typically this is not the case. Some facts are missing; thus, it is hard to arrive at an insightful synthesis. A factual representation of the situation is a truthful representation of the situation. Arriving at a factual description of the current state requires courage, and there are often vested interests that interfere. Good analysts are curious, critical, and candid. They can overcome the resistance from vested interests with a factual, clinical approach. You can say anything; it is all in the way you say it.

Strategic analysis requires a grid that is integrative of the whole enterprise. A model and a methodology to do this effectively are the subject of following sections in this chapter.

Such models and methodologies need to answer the question "Where are we?" The frequent and correct critique of strategic planning is that so much of it consists of endless analysis with little useful conclusions.

How much analysis is required? Enough to understand how the system works and why trends and results specific to the situation are occurring. The right level of analysis is the one that can explain what is going on. This is not a precise science; too little analysis can easily lead to loss of credibility, and too much takes the process outside the range of a strategic discussion and into something that is closer to budgeting.

Let us now address the design and development of a fact base that is adequate to the problem at hand.

2.2 Creating a Fact Base

A company's strategy says how it has chosen to adapt and exploit its environment. The purpose of a fact base is to understand the current strategy. At its most basic, it deals with three questions: (i) what are the dynamics in our environment, (ii) what is our current competitive position, and (iii) does our company have the requisite organization to successfully carry out its current strategy?

There are two broad sources of information to build a data base that will answer these questions.

The first is inside the company. The people who work there every day usually have the majority of the required information to do strategic analysis, but it is organized operationally in order to address day-to-day needs. Some of this information needs to be reformatted into a strategic framework for the purposes of a strategy-formulation process.

An effective and pragmatic way to do this is to proceed from questionnaires, interviews, and data searches onto development of an initial, tentative formulation of the strategy (sometimes referred to as a "straw man"). **Questionnaires** make it possible to cover much more ground than interviews ever can. And at the level of the enterprise, all the ground needs to be covered. An integrative tool, such as the High Performance Assessment™ described in a following section, can be a start in gathering the quantitative and qualitative inputs to access the genius inside. This can lead to the identification of a limited number of fundamental issues, usually five to seven of them. At this point, **individual interviews** are very effective to put "meat on the bone." From these interviews, a preliminary explanation or **straw man** can be developed to address the "how" and the "why" of the current strategy.

"Straw man" is a common language way to describe **prototyping**; at every step in the development of an idea, a product, or a strategy, try to define the "answer" based on the facts available to that point. It focuses the mind, promotes creativity, and identifies what is known and what has yet to be known.

Second, internal data should always be complemented with outside-in information. Why "always"? Because a natural bias is impossible to avoid. There is always some inbreeding, some tunnel vision, and changes occurring outside that have not yet been properly factored in.

Therefore, it is prudent to review **outside trends** and their potential impact. This is also true for **competitor analysis**. Even more interesting are **models of excellence**, companies or even institutions that, although they may be outside a company's immediate competitive set, nevertheless provide insight and objectivity in addressing current issues and future opportunities.

The test of a well-assembled fact base is as follows:

1. The ability of a reader to conclude that the **baseline forecast** shows a realistic picture of what to expect if current policies and strategies are maintained
2. The capacity to prepare a first attempt at answering the big question: What is the **opportunity** in this situation?

2.3   A Model of the Future-Creating Enterprise

A **model** synthesizes selected variables and the way in which they interact with one another according to certain principles. Models can thus be tested and improved through trial and error, as experience is accumulated.

Models are necessarily simplifications. They cannot fully correspond to a given reality. Still, they permit critical, mostly objective discussion about which competing representation provides the best target in a particular situation.

Looked at from the opposite angle, what happens if there is no enterprise model? In this case, one is left with diverse best practices that more or less fit together. This can lead to endless discussion about the superiority of competing elements. In the absence of a model there is a high probability of slower decisions and conflicting actions.

In addition, models provide a "decision framework" to assess the fit of various proposed initiatives. This can result in a significant economy of effort. Models also provide business leaders with a useful guidepost to assess progress through time.

The assumptions and principles that underlie our proposed model for the high performance enterprise are as follows:

- A consistent and coherent focus is superior to disparate initiatives, even in a turbulent environment.
- Business **leaders** must achieve two apparently conflicting goals at the same time: win today and create the future. The first requires discipline and consistency, while the second comes from radical thinking, creativity, and entrepreneurship.
- The organization with the highest motivation and commitment has a far better chance of winning in the end. Practices supporting a clear code create a high commitment culture. This must be grounded in a common belief system. Extreme individualism and the search for short-term maximized gains lead to cynicism and a lack of collaboration, the inverse of what, in essence, a high-performance organization requires.
- Superior models will inevitably emerge. The challenge, however, is to design and own them. This requires radical thinking in order to identify the shortcomings in current models and to seize the opportunities to build new ones.
- This is a long-term process. Building a future-creating enterprise requires solid foundations. It is a journey to mastery where the "quick fix" contributes little and may even dissipate acquired gains.

The future-creating enterprise must also have a world-class mindset: equal to the best or better and different than the best. Here are three ways to develop such a mindset:

- **Attitude:** "Good enough is not good enough." This is the true meaning of continuous improvement, year after year, relentlessly.

- **Benchmarking:** Benchmark a group of five to seven best companies that are related to your business to compare value-adding performance. This requires selecting the key indicators most pertinent in your industry and then comparing yourself to the average performance of these best performers.
- **Global mindset:** According to the previously cited IBM Global CEO study, the vast majority of financial outperformers (71 percent), are globalizers. This means that even companies that do not have a worldwide presence capitalize on global integration opportunities. They integrate differentiating capabilities, knowledge, and assets from around the world into **networked centers of excellence**. They have globally integrated business designs and detailed plans for partnering and M&A. They develop leaders that think and act globally. This includes developing social connections that improve integration and innovation.

Based on these principles and this mindset, the model proposed to build companies that can create a winning future addresses the two dimensions of the strategic problem and three foundations as follows:

1. **Winning today:** exploiting the advantage of dominating current markets.
2. **Creating the future:** new radical models to build new business opportunities.
3. **Organization and execution:** designing an organization to execute ① and ②.
4. **Change:** the capacity to make it happen with the required courage and resolve.
5. **Management leadership:** the motor and the impetus to design a winning model, execute it, maintain it, and strengthen it.

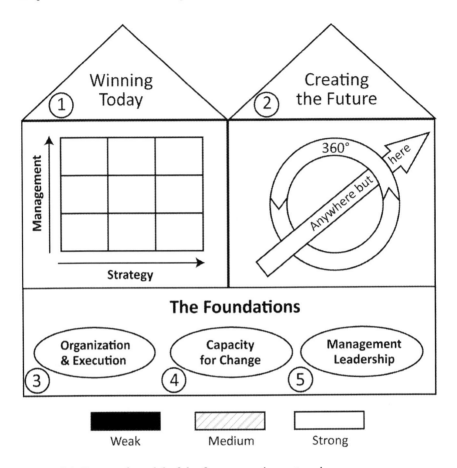

Figure 2.1. Proposed model of the future-creating enterprise.

2.4   The High Performance Assessment™

A good assessment of the current situation should start with an anonymous questionnaire that collects quantitative and qualitative inputs. Many such tools are available. In this section we describe the tool we have developed for this purpose, simply because it is the one we know. Please do not consider this as an advertisement. Rather, use this material to compare and validate the methodologies that are available to you through your network.

The High Performance Assessment™ is an enterprise-level methodology that tests some one hundred variables grouped in ten clusters, or dimensions. There are usually fifteen to fifty respondents.

They come from inside the company, because the questionnaire requires good knowledge of the company's or business unit's operations. The group of respondents does not need to be statistically representative. Indeed, when important changes are anticipated through the consulting process, it may be useful to select a group of "best and brightest" participants. This creates a powerful lever in the subsequent consulting process to ask questions such as, "Our survey group sees (x). What do you think?"

The application of a High Performance Assessment results in a factual description of the current state and enables discussions and decisions about the real situation:

- It provides an elaborate, fact-based **assessment** of the current situation based on the perception of responding managers.
- It minimizes subjectivity, biases, and defensiveness by using an **anonymous, objective format.**

The High Performance Assessment achieves this because it is based on a rational enterprise model, which creates a neutral discussion framework. The report produced at the end of the assessment addresses issues, not personalities.

As an added benefit, participants are asked to propose items for immediate improvements. This list, compiled by the company's best and brightest people, typically produces results far in excess of the costs required to apply the High Performance Assessment.

Here is how a client, Pat Mitchell, then president and COO of Cold Spring Granite in Cold Spring, Minnesota, applied and leveraged this methodology.

> *Before the assessment, we had assumptions about what we were doing and how our people really thought of us, but we had no way to quantify it.*
>
> *The assessment was a shock. We had respectable scores for operational excellence and for the work environment, but we were not customer focused, compared to a world-class high performance organization. I have to say I was surprised at how far away we are from the scores of real high-growth*

companies.

What was amazing was how the assessment energized us. We are now able to identify root causes as to why our growth strategies have not been successful, and what we need to do to change that. To achieve growth, we know now that we must create a culture that supports high performance. Not only do we need to be customer focused, but we need to work on people development to create an internal structure that encourages performance, agree on strategy, and distinguish between the roles of leadership and management.

The High Performance Assessment has rocked the culture of this company. We looked in that mirror and saw not just that we needed to change but how to accomplish it.

Figure 2.2 A and B present the final integration and synthesis of the High Performance Assessment, the conclusion which addresses the "so what?" question after one hundred variables have been measured. The data in Figure 2.2 is from an actual client situation. This company had strong and even dominant positions in some of its market segments, but profitability and returns were below average. A strong company with below average financial performance. A highly collaborative, "can do" culture, but strategies that were too disparate and inefficient use of capital. There was a lot of upside potential, but first the company had to become a tighter ship.

Figure 2.2A starts with our model of the future-creating enterprise as presented previously in section 2.3. Results for each of the five components are color coded to represent a weak, medium, or strong evaluation. In the questionnaire, two types of questions are asked: (i) questions of evaluation, which use a scale of 1 to 5, and (ii) questions of positioning, which are based on the percent of respondents that agree or disagree. In our client example, two components of the model were judged to be good and three to be strong:

- **Winning today** regroups questions on business goals, strategy and client-driven. Average score was 3.9. This is good and very close to strong on the scale of 1 to 5, where a score of 4.0 and up is superior, 3.5 to 3.9 is good, and 3.4 or less is weak.

- **Creating the future** is evaluated by questions on innovation. This score was 4.0.
- **Organization and execution** is analyzed through structure, operational excellence, management processes, people processes, and motivation. Total average score was 3.8.
- **Change** is assessed by participants' view of whether the company's past behavior was proactive or reactive. Past behavior is a strong predictor of future behavior. The fact that 87.0% of respondents judged the company to be proactive was a very positive sign that required changes would be successfully implemented.
- Finally, **management and leadership** were evaluated at 4.1.

The company's overall score was 3.9 was good to strong.

On figure 2.2B are answers from participants to questions on positioning. 91 percent of respondents think the company will grow in the future. 70 percent think the present situation is satisfactory. The next questions deal with the participants' position on what to do about this and their suggestions of what other companies can provide as a model of excellence that can inspire our efforts to move forward.

The challenge in this case is to raise the bar, to increase discipline in a situation that is already successful, and, truth be told, comfortable.

Company leaders are presented with the results of this self-assessment. They are asked to discuss this picture of the present situation in small breakout groups and to address the question "Is this us?" It is hard to refute a picture that has been created by a group of respondents that were chosen by oneself. Once the picture is agreed, the first step in a process to create the future is completed.

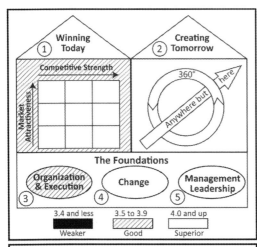

① **Winning Today**

- Business Goals   4.2
- Business Strategy   3.5
- Client Driven   <u>4.1</u>
  - Good   <u>3.9</u>

② **Creating Tomorrow**

- Innovation   <u>4.0</u>
  - Superior   <u>4.0</u>

③ **Organization and Execution**

- Structure   3.7
- Oper. Excellence   3.5
- Management Processes   3.7
- People Processes   3.8
- Motivation   4.0
- Satisfaction   <u>3.9</u>
  - Good   <u>3.8</u>

④ **Change**

- Proactive   <u>87.0%</u>
  - Superior   <u>87.0%</u>

⑤ **Management Leadership**

- Leadership   <u>4.1</u>
  - Superior   <u>4.1</u>

Average Total Score: 3.9

The average total score is an indication of a company's total strength. But it must be understood in the context of the stronger and weaker categories as indicated to the right of this page.

Figure 2.2A – Summary of Results: the Big Picture

Baseline Forecast	**Is this satisfactory?**
1) grow 91.3% 2) stable 8.7% 3) decline 0%	1) Yes 69.6% 2) No 30.4%

3 Top Moves	**3 Key Barriers**

• Acquisitions (8) *
 • People/leadership dev. (4)
 • Expand business definition (4)
    - Competitive overheads, developer, general
     contractor, contractor in new complex products
    - Create/manage the future
 • Revisit B.U. structure (2)
	• Finance (5)
	 • Culture/attitude (5)
	    - Low cooperation, paradigms, acquisition
	     integration, managing the future
	 • Weakening performance (4)
	    - Loss in market share, loss of key employees,
	     major projects going wrong

External Models of Excellence	**Immediate Action**
• AAA (3) • None (3) • BBB (2) • CCC: mastery of acquisition integration (1) • DDD: op. excellence and innovation (1) • FFF, GGG, HHH	• Improve innovation, new product process (4) • Define and achieve N.A. Segment B leadership (2) • Acquisition integration process (1) • More efficient Engineering (1) • Global sourcing and fabrication (1) • Mandatory use of Skype for long distance calls (1)

* Indicates number of mentions

Figure 2.2B – What do you think we should do?

Figure 2.2 A and Figure 2.2 B

2.5   Validation

The question of validation addresses the trustworthiness and usefulness of the assessment process.

The High Performance Assessment™ is a tool that provides the foundation for a company's or a business unit's strategic planning process. Each situation is unique, and the pertinent question is "What is our specific problem?" This is answered when client managers review the test result in a workshop and decide that "this indeed, is us." The test can then be said to be **factual**.

The test is based on a documented model that provides the **theory** to support it. This is the purpose of this book: integrate the best theory and the best examples into a practical framework for business leaders.

Because the test is based on a standard model, it is also **reproducible**. Companies can use it at regular periods over time to measure progress, and they can use it in different business units to measure alignment.

As a first step in a consulting process, the High Performance Assessment™ provides **real outcomes** for immediate improvements (low-hanging fruit), strategic decisions, organization development, major business process transformations, and team coaching.

Test scores follow the **normal distribution curve**. A sufficiently large sample—fifteen to fifty participants who answer more than one hundred questions anonymously—leads to truthful results that are then further validated through individual interviews and group workshops. Insightful data, criticized and validated by the company's own leaders, always creates powerful results.

The test is applied by trained and certified consultants.

Chapter 3: The Genius Is Inside

3.1   A Design Template for the Requisite Organization

What is the organization that can best deliver a future-creating strategy?

It is the organization that provides the opportunity for each of its members to contribute to his or her full potential. The starting point of organization design is people, highly motivated people. This level of motivation is created by clarity of responsibility and relationships, existence of the required skills and tools, autonomy of execution, fact-based assessment of performance, and fair rewards.

The template illustrated in figure 3.1 will be used to discuss and present the elements that are proposed to design a future creating organization: flat, lean structures complemented with project management, as well as on-the-ground execution networks or teams, aligned business processes, and a culture of high standards. More specifically, the components of the template are as follows:

- Resources and business processes that will provide superior capacity to execute the organization's **strategy** for winning today and creating the future.
- Superb execution of **tasks of excellence**, which are the essence of a differentiated position in its domain; the one or two characteristics or functions that create a recognized competitive advantage in a company's business sector.

The strategy and the tasks of excellence should be the design criteria for the organization. The actual components that constitute the organization that will meet these criteria are as follows:

- **A structure** that balances centralization and decentralization and allocates resources dynamically to the most critical success areas.
- **Business processes**, such as strategic planning, continuous improvement, human capital, and information management that work together to create a high-performance management system.
- **A culture** that provides the glue to hold things together and pull the company forward.
- **People** that have a high degree of ownership and motivation; people that not only do their job but also participate in building the company.

This chapter will present a target state for an organization capable of delivering a future-creating strategy.

The city of Paris provides a good example for using a target state model to create the future. In the late nineteenth century, Baron Haussmann was responsible for rebuilding the city with the overarching aim to make it the most beautiful in the world. The target design, with its large, open boulevards, also provided the authorities with a powerful way to control the armed rebellions that were prevalent at the time. How was this achieved?

- First, the future city, the model, was designed (i.e., the "plan d'urbanisme").
- Second, what fit the model was kept, of course.
- Third, the rest was gradually replaced.
- Finally, and most importantly, all future decisions and actions fit into the plan.

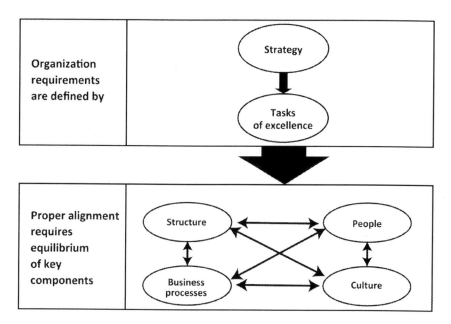

Figure 3.1. Organization design template.

3.2   Lean, Aligned, and Learning Structures

It is generally accepted that a hierarchy is required, and there has been much research on the type and complexity of the most appropriate organizational designs. Despite all this research, there are very few hard conclusions. Our bias is to focus on structures that favor high motivation. Structures deal mostly with the organization of current work. They need to be complemented with project structures that address process improvement and future creating initiatives. The following principles will help to design the specific structure required for a given organization.

- **Minimalist hierarchy.** Clearly, too many companies have been badly served by too many levels of hierarchy. An excessive number of levels leads to slowness and lack of initiative—not a winning formula. So, how much hierarchy is required? Basically, this is determined by the number of time spans that have to be managed. Typically, operating employees manage a time span of hours or days. The next level up should deal in months and further levels with increasing number of years. Different problems come with different time spans. When the structure is designed to make sure that overlap is maintained at the strictest minimum required to insure integration, cooperation and respect increase, and turf wars are minimized. Elliot Jaques proposes that seven levels should be the maximum that any large organization requires. Nucor, to be discussed later, has four levels in their operating units. This is possible because of the extensive use of **teams** that are in business for themselves at the operating level. These self-managed teams form a **network** where operating decisions are assumed by the people who do the work, thus reducing significantly the need for high levels of direct supervision.

- **Focus on the main game**. Most structures actually do not address this correctly. Lt. General William G. Pagonis explained it well. In any given situation, there is one activity that clearly constitutes the "battle front." Clearly, in a war situation, it is the frontline soldier. Lt. General Pagonis makes the point that all the rest is support and that the contribution of all these support functions needs to be assessed in terms of their impact on this most critical dimension.

  This concept provides a useful design guideline in non-military situations. For example:

  - In a product-driven company, such as a car manufacturer, product development, sales, and service are the areas of excellence.
  - In a consumer marketing company, market research and branding are critical.
  - In a technology company, it will be research and applications marketing.
  - In a production company, it will be manufacturing efficiency and marketing focused on replacing competing products.
  - In a distribution company, it will be a unique system or method, operations management.

- **Learning and innovation through project approach.** The hierarchical structure deals with the present. Improvements to the current business model, incremental innovation and creation of the future, and radical innovation are essential and need their own methodology. This is provided by **project approaches** and **knowledge systems**. The key is to see these two methodologies as an integral part of a company's structure. Projects provide a great opportunity for individuals to use their creativity. Motivation and commitment of the project teams are in direct relationship with the level of effective project management.

When combined together, these elements form the **"hypertext" organization**, as presented in figure 3.2. As illustrated, three structures actually coexist and feed into one another at the same time:

- **The business-system** layer is where current, routine operations are carried out: "winning today." This is the traditional hierarchical structure, but it should be lean.
- **The project-team** layer is where multiple project teams engage in knowledge creating activities, such as new product development. This is where tomorrow is created.
- **The knowledge-base** layer is where the organizational knowledge developed in the two previous layers is categorized and contextualized. This layer does not exist as an actual organizational entity but is embedded in corporate vision, intellectual property, organizational culture, and technology.

In such a hypertext framework, the members of the organization can move from one context to another. Learning and innovation opportunities are multiplied and individual development is given the greatest number of opportunities. But most importantly, vested interests are minimized. Everyone understands that there are different jobs to be done that require specific, adapted skills.

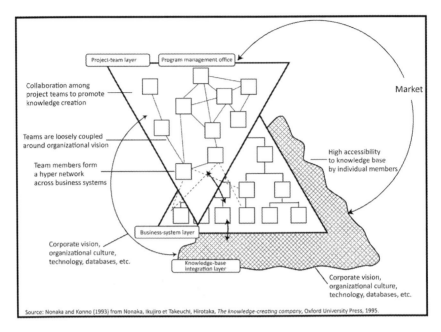

Figure 3.2. The hypertext framework.

Structures can always be improved, and assessments should be regular. Have we achieved our "Paris plan d'urbanisme"? If not, what is the gap between our current structure and the target structure?

These more detailed questions could help with this assessment:

- Does the structure direct adequate management resources to each target market segment?
- Are responsibility and accountability clearly defined?
- Do units receive the requisite support to carry out their mandates?
- Is coordination between units simple?
- Is decision making closest to the action?
- Is knowledge shared seamlessly?
- Is project management effective?
- Where appropriate are teams used very effectively?
- Is the organization lean?

Companies that get in trouble often restructure. They believe this will solve their problem. Most often this is wrong. If the structure fits the needs of the situation, the basic design should not change when times are bad. A truthful diagnostic should usually reveal more important levers for improvement.

3.3   Four-Wheel-Drive Business Processes

Business processes are linked activities that produce a result for the company. They cut across structures, and they are often seen as horizontal, whereas structures are typically vertical. Business processes can be strategic, such as business planning, or very operational, such as accounts receivable collection. Business processes in most companies offer a gold mine of improvement potential.

In this section, we will deal with selected business processes that provide high-level corporate-wide impact to illustrate what value they should provide and how they can work together, when they are well designed, to complement and reinforce each other. In other words, they provide the company with a four-wheel-drive management system. A system that continuously builds performance and innovation capabilities.

a.   **Strategic planning** is first a performance discipline. At the level of **alignment**, it provides the discipline to strengthen focus, create superior organic growth, and achieve cost competitiveness. The strategic planning process is the forum where the goals and action plans are agreed and monitored.

Incremental innovation builds on this alignment process. It is itself a systematic process with clear goals and methodologies.

Radical innovation is the third leg of the strategic planning process. It stands apart from the previous two, because it requires another point of view, very different lenses to look at reality. Still, a company that is strong in the first two aspects provides the most fertile ground for radical innovation.

A strategic planning process that provides these three streams of ideas and actions is truly at the center of creating a company's future.

b. Continuous-improvement processes are the perfect complement to strategic planning processes. Strategic planning deals with medium- and longer-term issues. Strategic planning mainly involves the more senior levels of the organization. Continuous improvement is a CEO decision, because it greatly impacts competitive strength and organization culture. Continuous improvement deals with daily work and happens at the first level of operations.

As Anand Sharma of the TBM Consulting Group explains it: continuous improvement aims for lean operations (i.e., the elimination of waste). This needs to be coordinated centrally to ensure that the company invests its time and efforts on well-thought-through priorities. Typically, there is a "Kaizen Promotion Office."

Lean operating systems involve a philosophy and a number of tools. Lean operating systems are derived from the Toyota Manufacturing System. The heart of the approach is the Kaizen event. Kaizen means continuous incremental improvement involving everyone, including both managers and workers. Kaizen is a philosophy that assumes that our way of life (working, social, or private) deserves to be constantly improved.

Lean operations concepts can be integrated with six-sigma quality approaches. Lean is typically seen as a bottom-up approach and deals with "what you see." Six-sigma is very effective in process situations and with problems of yield, for example. All these approaches started on the manufacturing shop floor, but they have since migrated to business processes in manufacturing companies and from there to service and professional organizations.

So how do you create a lean organization? James P. Womack and Daniel T. Jones present an excellent summary using Pratt & Whitney as a case in point:

> The most obvious is to begin with what you do right now. Don't think about what your workforce doesn't know, their lack of education, or their age. Don't think about the past obstructions of your union or the

need for good quarterly numbers. These barriers exist mainly in your own head.

Instead, line up your value-creating activities in a continuous flow to improve quality while taking out large blocks of cost. This can be accomplished quickly if you have the knowledge—it has taken three years in the massive Pratt production system, which provides the toughest possible test—and it never requires significant sums for new equipment or plant. As costs fall, freeing up resources for new initiatives, it is much easier to see what to do next, including up-skilling your workforce. Indeed, a fundamentally different cost structure for existing operations will often suggest a very different strategy from what would have been pursued if the old cost structure had been taken as a given. (Pratt, for example, could never have dreamed of competing in the engine overhaul business with its pre-1992 cost structure)...

In any case, by starting with what it does now, Pratt has dramatically reduced its costs while pleasing its customers. As a result, operating results rebounded from losses of $283 million in 1992 and $262 million in 1993 to profits of $380 million in 1994 and $530 million in 1995, even as sales continued to sag. Pratt has bought the time needed to complete the introduction of lean principles across the business and given itself considerable latitude in deciding what to do next.

Creating a lean organization is not a straightforward proposition. If you are going to do it for real, this represents a transformational change, with all that this involves: people who don't get it; early pitfalls, which provide an excuse to quit; and going at it superficially, which can achieve improvements but not world-class competitiveness. This is a true test of leadership.

A robust-continuous improvement process will achieve superior-quality cost competitiveness, and it will create the fertile ground for incremental innovation.

c. **High-commitment people practices** insure that, in addition to doing their jobs well, committed people will provide the organization with their brains and their creativity. The gap between such an environment and one where people are lukewarm or even antagonistic is immense. The potential of an organization with highly committed people is almost limitless.

This does not happen by chance. First and foremost, there has to be a clear contract between the company and its people. Put simply, in order to get more, you have to give more. This requires long-term security and a clear code, supported with integrity on the company's part, good work, and creative participation on the individual's part.

Second, **get the right people on the bus**, as Jim Collins put it in *Good to Great*. Working and developing people who have a mindset that is in agreement with the goal is highly productive.

Trying to realign someone who is going in a different direction is very unproductive for the individual and the company. Operationally, the hiring decision is probably the most important of all.

The main characteristics of high-performance organizations have been well summarized by John Roberts (*The Modern Firm*, referenced in bibliography) as follows:

> The model of "high commitment human resource management systems" presents a general example of using several different elements of PARC (people, architecture, routines, culture) to achieve motivation. Key elements of such systems include guaranteed employment (except for egregious behaviour); egalitarian values and norms; **self-managed** teams for organizing production; attempts to make work interesting and fulfilling; **premium compensation**, perhaps involving team, unit, or firm-wide (but not individual) performance pay; rigorous pre-employment screening and extensive socialization and training of employees; **transparency of information** within the firm and open **communication channels between employees** and managers, a strong culture focused on

an **overarching goal** such as the organization's vision; and a strong emphasis on employees symbolic and financial **"ownership" of the firm.** The basic deal is that people work hard and cleverly, in the interests of the firm in return for good pay, empowerment, trust, and interesting, fulfilling work... mutual monitoring and social pressure among employees enforce the desired behaviours. The screening, socialization, and identification with the vision help ensure that the **enforcement mechanisms are at work**.

A company that achieves this level of high performance will have the best people in each job, it will create its future leadership, and it will have lean, high-impact management. It will be an employer of choice.

d. **Innovation,** both incremental and radical, is the specific tool of entrepreneurs. Through innovation, they exploit changes or discontinuities as an opportunity for creating a new product or a new service. An innovation is an increase of the performance on the yield on resources; an innovation also changes the value and satisfaction obtained from resources by the customer.

Systematic innovation consists of an organized, disciplined search for changes as well as the identification of opportunities for increasing value for the customer. In the realm of innovation, managers have access to practices that have been demonstrated to be effective. The rate of success at innovating may be lower or higher in different companies, depending on the practices and entrepreneurship talents that are brought to bear; nevertheless, innovation always entails a real risk of failure.

A first step in the quest for continuous innovation is to establish categories. This serves two important purposes: it prevents people acting toward contrary ends, and it focuses efforts (the necessary condition to achieve real results). If, for example, you do not see the radical innovation category, you will very likely miss it completely. In our work with clients, we find it useful to propose three categories of innovation, each involving different conditions and dynamics: incremental innovation, radical innovation, and invention. Each requires a specific distinct approach. This is similar to strategic market-segment analysis, where each segment is defined as having a specific set of products, clients and competitors, thus requiring a particular strategy.

What is it that differentiates incremental and radical innovation? The level of novelty and the quantum of wealth creation are different, from somewhat (say 10 to 50 percent) to a lot (say five to ten times).

- **Incremental innovation.** This deals with products for the most part, but it also includes technology, continuous improvement, and processes. These objects of innovation fit well together because they lend themselves to a similar group of management methodologies and are effective in the context of a supportive organization culture.
  Product innovations, for example, were analyzed by Booz Allen and Hamilton in 1982 and grouped as follows:[1]

  - Cost reductions (11%)
  - Repositionings (7%)
  - Revision/improvements to existing products (26%)
  - Additions to existing product lines (26%)
  - New product lines (20%)
  - New-to-the-world products (10%)

The processes that facilitate and nurture incremental innovation are typically applied to the current organization and its people. It is the leader's job to set up the game, but the bulk of the

---

[1] Kotler, Philip, and Ronald E. Turner, *Marketing Management* (Englewood Cliffs, NJ: Prentice-Hall, 1989), page 312.

result will ultimately come from bottom-up inputs. Obviously, incremental innovation is a great team builder.

- **Radical innovation.** This deals with new space and new rules. In both cases it may touch the enterprise system and the culture as a whole.

  New space involves new market space. It requires a new and different configuration of product attributes and often leads to the creation of an entirely new category. New rules apply to the management model of enterprise, its organization.

  New space and new rules, because they affect the whole enterprise, not only need senior management leadership, but often they are also executed by senior management.

- **Invention is discovery.** It is often the result of looking for something, making an error, and stumbling upon a discovery. Sometimes it is the fruit of one individual's efforts, possibly working alone against the established system. Other times, it comes from ad hoc project teams or structured R&D.

  Clearly, invention is not programmable to the same extent as incremental innovation and radical innovation. But companies that are innovative and creative will be in the best position to provide a productive haven for the inventor and help him to bring invention to the market.

3.4   Culture: The Best Idea Wins

The previous sections of this chapter have addressed structural and system elements of the requisite organization. But structures and systems alone will not do it. There needs to be a "glue" to make things stick together and to pull them forward.

An overarching value or a set of closely related values will provide the organization with a code, a philosophy, a system of beliefs that will guide long-term choices and daily behavior. Values define who we are and why we are in this organization together. An authentic set of values will create trust, allow autonomy, and increase collaboration and teamwork. Value statements can easily be just hot air. In these situations, they often produce negative results. Better not to bother.

So how can appropriate values be identified? By understanding the problem at hand. Values are a decision guideline, so in order to be real and credible, values must be related and useful in the situation. Then they help in taking rational decisions, in submitting options to critical thinking; they define a company's non-negotiable items.

In a company that aims to create its future, **performance today** and **creating the future** are the critical problems. What values can help to achieve superior results in each of these dimensions? High performance, innovation, and creativity are driven by the aspiration to be the best, to create something new: the goal is to encourage people to be curious, critical, creative, and constructive. Such qualities flourish when the code is that the **best idea wins**, always.

This in turn creates emulation and maturity. Participants in an environment where the best idea wins need to be able to "leave their egos at the door" and rally to the best idea. No one has a veto. This may not be for everyone. Yet most people will rise to the occasion if they are given the chance. People can mature and get used to being one team always based on trust, openness, and integrity. This is a leadership challenge.

A final note. The above is a plea against consensus, an approach that usually leads an organization to decline. The reason is mathematical. Under "the best idea wins," the company always gets 100 percent of the best solutions. Under consensus, it gets 75 percent or less of the best answers. This destroys the competitive edge, if there was one in the first place.

3.5   Creating a Virtuous Circle

When the elements of a high performance organization are working together a virtuous circle is created. Each element feeds and reinforces the others. As the wheel turns, the system actually moves upwards in terms of efficiency, strength, performance. Psychologists call this **appreciative enquiry**.

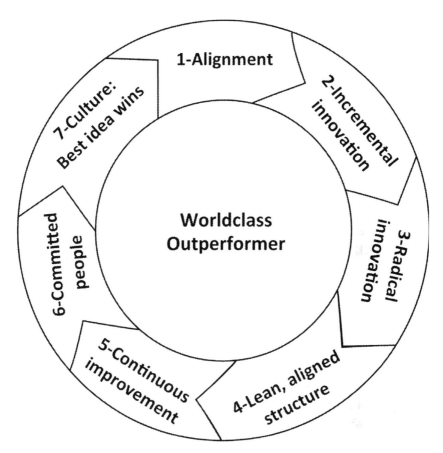

Figure 3.3. A virtuous circle of high performance.

3.6   The Nucor Example

Ken Iverson, chairman of Nucor Corporation (1965–1998) described their competitive strategy as follows: "Our competitive strategy is to build manufacturing facilities economically and to operate them efficiently—period."

Nucor's manufacturing assets are located strategically to optimize client service and logistics. The company seeks to beat rivals by using advanced—and often unproven—processes to produce high-quality steel at the lowest possible cost. Its productivity, as measured by man-hours per ton, is eight times greater than the best traditional integrated mills.

Nucor's management philosophy is even more radical than

its approach to technology. The company is highly decentralized with most day-to-day operating decisions made by the division general managers and their staff. Typical divisions have only three management levels, in addition to hourly employees:

- General manager
- Department manager
- Supervisor/professional
- Hourly employee

Employee relations at Nucor are based on four clear-cut principles:

1. Management is obliged to manage Nucor in such a way that employees will have the opportunity to earn according to their productivity.
2. Employees should be able to feel confident that if they do their jobs properly, they will have a job tomorrow.
3. Employees have the right to be treated fairly and must believe that they will be.
4. Employees must have an avenue of appeal when they believe they are being treated unfairly.

By implementing these four basic principles within a relatively simple organizational structure, Nucor has been able to attract and retain highly talented and productive employees.

Performance-Based Compensation

Nucor provides employees with a performance-related compensation system that rewards goal-oriented individuals. All employees are covered under one of four basic compensation plans, each featuring incentives related to meeting specific goals and targets.

1. *Production Incentive Plan:* Operation and maintenance employees and supervisors are paid weekly bonuses, based on the productivity of their work group. The rate is calculated based on the capabilities of the equipment employed, and

no bonus is paid if the equipment is not operating. The Production Incentive bonus can average from 80 to 150 percent of an employee's base pay.

2. *Department Manager Incentive Plan:* Department managers earn annual incentive bonuses, based primarily on the percentage of net income to dollars of assets employed, for their division. These bonuses can be as much as 80 percent of a department manager's base pay.

3. *Professional and Clerical Bonus Plan:* This bonus is paid to employees who are not on the production or department manager plan and is based on the division's net income return on assets.

4. *Senior Officers Incentive Plan:* Nucor's senior officers do not have employment contracts. They do not participate in any pension, discretionary bonus, or retirement plans. Their base salaries are set lower than what executives receive in comparable companies. The remainder of their compensation is based on Nucor's annual overall percentage of net income to stockholder's equity and is paid out in cash and stock.

In addition to these established bonus plans, Nucor has periodically issued an extraordinary bonus to all employees, except officers, in years of particularly strong company performance.

Egalitarian Benefits

Nucor takes an egalitarian approach to providing benefits to its employees. That is to say, the upper levels of management do not enjoy better insurance programs, vacation schedules, or holidays. In fact, certain benefits, such as Nucor's Profit Sharing, Scholarship Program, Employee Stock Purchase Plan, Extraordinary Bonus, and Service Awards Program, are not available to Nucor's officers. Senior executives do not enjoy traditional perquisites, such as company cars, corporate jets, executive dining rooms, or executive parking places.

Nucor's egalitarian culture places a premium on teamwork and idea-sharing between frontline workers and management. Result: A highly profitable partnership.		
Pay for Performance	»	On average, two-thirds of a Nucor steelworker's pay is based on a production bonus, with profit-sharing layered on top of that. It can be a lucrative formula, but the risks are real. In 2005 the typical worker received $91,293; three years earlier a steel slump left workers with $58,931. CEO and executive pay is similarly tied to performance targets.
Listen to the Front Line	»	Execs say almost all of the best ideas come from the factory floor—and the newest workers often come up with them. In the wake of its recent acquisitions, Nucor is sending new workers to existing plants to hunt for improvement opportunities and having older workers see what they can learn from newly acquired plants.
Push-Down Authority	»	To minimize layers of management, Nucor has pushed work that used to be done by supervisors, such as ordering parts, down to line workers, and push the duties of plant managers down to supervisors. CEO DiMicco says his executive vice-presidents are like "mini CEOs, and I'm their board".
Protect Your Culture	»	As Nucor grows, protecting its egalitarian philosophy and team spirit is more of a challenge. A decentralized structure helps, but management makes cultural compatibility a big focus of its acquisition research. In visits to potential acquisitions, careful attention is paid to how plant workers and managers interact.
Try Unproven Technologies	»	Forays into new technologies haven't always paid off for Nucor, but it realizes the importance of taking risks. One project to make wire from steel failed miserably, and a $200 million attempt to build up a supply of raw materials in the Carribean had to be scrapped. But successes such as thin slab casting of sheet metal have made Nucor an industry leader

Figure 3.4. Forging a winning workforce.

Source: Nanette Byrnes, "The Art of Motivation," *Business Week*, May 1, 2006.

Chapter 4: Alignment

4.1   A Client Example: "Crossing the Desert"

On paper, the questions of alignment are simple. "How many businesses have you got?" and "Do you have dedicated resources to deal with each business?" The reality is often significantly more opaque. Here is a client example that illustrates the impact of proper organizational alignment.

I. The Business/the Organization

This client is a steel manufacturer who supplies the construction industry with structures, joists, bridges, prefabricated buildings, and flooring systems. By the year 2000, sales had reached $1 billion and the company operated in North America and Europe. This client, from a very small base, had become an industry leader over a period of twenty-five years under the leadership of the founder. The company was seen as entrepreneurial, its profit performance was good, and its stock performed well.

Then trouble hit. The market tanked, as is proverbial in the construction industry. This exacerbated internal problems, which had slowly taken form over the previous expansion cycle. The time had also come to transfer management leadership to the next generation. The new president faced a double challenge: put the business back on course, building on a strong culture, but at the same time create a new spirit of focus and performance in a team used to winning, but now playing a "losing season."

II. The Challenge

This was a well established company with a very strong reputation for superior client service. It enjoyed the number one or two position in most of its markets. But this success led to over-diversification, diminished focus, and a number of business lines or internal activities that were not earning their way. In order to move forward, the following requirements were agreed upon:

- Refocus and restructure the business.
- Identify growth opportunities with low capital requirements.
- Align the cost structure to the new business profile.
- Increase accountability for results.
- Establish a strong follow-up discipline.

The business definition was clear. What was required was **alignment** and **accountability**. This market dominator, which had over diversified, needed to renew its entrepreneurship in terms of mindset to become the challenger again.

III. The Approach

A fact base was created using methodologies such as the High Performance Assessment™, external models of excellence, and internal interviews. When the results were discussed in early workshops with a group of approximately thirty senior managers, it became painfully apparent that the same data could be seen from two opposing perspectives. For some, the data simply documented the challenges the company had to address. For others, the information was seen as a threat and it created defensive behavior.

The president and the consulting team decided to avoid more discussion on the fact base; after all, the data was on the table. Instead, the process was organized around two of the critical outputs that were accepted by all: how to find growth after a period of industry consolidation and severe downsizing, and what needed to be done to align costs to a downsized business base.

Two teams were created to deal with each question: the "Air Force" and the "Marines." They were given five weeks to get the job done. Both were successful.

A major improvement opportunity appeared around two questions: "How many businesses are there in this company?" and "Does each have a dedicated leader?" The numbers didn't match. Upon review, all businesses were found to have good to great potential. There was no justification for the orphan treatment given to half the business sectors under current arrangements. Redesigning the structure so that each business had dedicated resources with very clear targets led to predictably improved results in terms of sales, market position, and profits.

From this organization realignment followed targeted business plans and dedicated execution. Entrepreneurship, which had been located at the CEO level for the most part, was recreated at the business unit level. Many challenges surfaced. Not all businesses were mature. The drivers of some were different from these of others. Gradually, "one size fits all" changed to targeted strategies, execution, and metrics.

IV. The Value Delivered

Over the following twelve-month period, sales from ongoing activities increased 14 percent and profits from ($5.9 million) to $38.6 million, a $44.5-million turnaround. The stock has doubled.

Having put its core business back on a high performing and successful path, the company is now addressing the next level of strategy, the creation of an innovative future. On the agenda are issues of innovation processes, client relationships, and renewed management models.

Based on this example, this chapter will discuss concepts that are the foundations of efficient and effective alignment: "maturity," differentiated competitive advantage, competitive spirit, and the strategy formulation process.

4.2   The Problem of "Maturity"

Mature businesses are those that have always been average or those whose superior performance at one time has now flattened out. There can be many reasons for this, and they can feed into one another.

- Past growth could have been driven by acquisitions, and they somehow cannot be repeated.
- As Richard Pasquale has pointed out, "Nothing fails like success." Great strengths are at the root of great weaknesses as the environment and the competitive set changes. People work hard in these companies, but they are focused on doing more and better of the wrong business model.
- Finally, managers may simply be uncomfortable in setting demanding targets. It is much easier to go along with "good enough is good enough" thinking. Setting demanding goals creates a risk to one's reputation and relationships. ("What if things do not work out? / Who does this guy think he is?")

The problem of maturity can be overcome. It requires the capacity for superior organic growth, the critical thinking required to change the business model as required, the courage to ask for high results, and the entrepreneurship to take risks on new initiatives. In concrete terms, opportunities for growth will be found at three different levels of strategy, from lower risk to higher risk.

1. **Alignment.** Alignment aims to do more and better with the same. This is the lowest risk, most profitable approach. It should be exploited fully. This is the subject of the current chapter.
2. **Incremental innovation.** This is the domain of new initiatives that are complementary to the current business model. This is medium risk. It is the subject of chapter 5.
3. **Radical innovation.** This involves new space, new rules. The business model is reinvented. The risks are possibly higher, but eventually all companies need to reinvent themselves. This is chapter 6.

In most situations, there is no such thing as a mature business. To keep it growing, it is logical and prudent to start with alignment. There is usually, and always somewhat surprisingly, a lot of potential in there. It requires strategic marketing (i.e., a differentiated position), superior salesmanship (i.e., competitive spirit), and a process that sets high standards and follows-up with iron discipline (i.e., *strategic* strategic planning).

We will start with differentiation.

4.3   A Differentiated Competitive Advantage

For the ancient Greeks, strategy was the "art of the general." A combination of the elements at hand to create a winning stratagem or plan.

One word that keeps coming up in definitions and discussions of strategy is **clever** (e.g., "The most clever plan wins"). Clever in turn requires sufficient **insight** to propose something **different** that creates superior value. Most companies do not have a clever, differentiated plan:

- In the worst cases, companies have unfocussed strategies and disparate organizational practices. Most of the effort inside these companies is wasted. Such a company could be called a "**house of pain.**"
- Others have thought things through. They have a definition of their business, of what they sell to whom; they have made choices of priority market segments and they have a game plan for each. What prevents them from being the leader is that they bring nothing new to the party; they follow the current rules instead of being entrepreneurial and reinventing them. They are competent, but they are in the middle; they are **rule takers**.
- High strategic performers set the rules. They benefit from all the advantages of such a position: privileged client relationships, advanced technologies, the best people, the best margins. They are the **rule makers**. Andrew Campbell discusses the requisite insight to be a rule maker as follows:

The key to a good strategy is a good insight about how to create more value than competitors. An insight is an understanding, normally about some pretty detailed issues **that is sufficiently practical to point to a new way of doing things** – a superior way. The insight can be about the relationship with suppliers, about the details of the recruitment process or the needs of a particular group of employees, about a segment of customers, and about the value equation being used by shareholders. Sometimes the insight is a grand idea to completely reconfigure the company or the industry. More normally it is a discovery that some process can be operated with fewer people or that some customers require a particular additional service. The very nature of insight means that it is usually possessed by a certain line or operating manager who may not be fully aware of its significance. Without the insights, objectives are unachievable, missions are dreams, and tactics fail.

Analysis is necessary to create good insights, but it does not lead to it directly. **Creativity** is the bridge between **strategic analysis** and **strategic thinking**. Henry Mintzberg has made the point forcefully that strategic planning is not strategic thinking. Strategic analysis provides the feedstock required for strategic thinking. In the best conditions, the one we are presenting in this book, strategic planners understand this distinction, support managers in their creative process, and can actually contribute to the discussion and the definition of a differentiated competitive advantage.

4.4   Competitive Spirit

Clever ideas are necessary, but they are not sufficient. There are many examples of someone's clever idea that became the source of somebody else's great wealth and success. Remember the classic example of the microwave oven, which was invented by Amana but successfully developed and marketed by Japanese manufacturers.

Competitive spirit is what provides the drive to transform clever ideas into dominant market positions or to achieve and maintain dominant positions in the current business.

If you have been in the military, or if you practice a discipline that involves combat (boxing or martial arts, for example), you know that all the preparation, all the training, is essential, but that the truth is ultimately created through **combat**. In combat there is a winner and a loser.

Competition is the business equivalent of war. It requires techniques and disciplines. With that said, there is no preset formula to achieve competitive superiority. Similarly to strategy in general, it is your mindset and insight that make the difference.

Actually, competition is the unique role of business in our society. Boxers and karate fighters aim for the knockout punch. Highly competitive companies look to achieve the same result against their competitors. This is actually very valuable to all concerned. It is highly motivating to management and employees. Working for a winner brings the greatest rewards and security. The dynamic is good even for competitors, who are forced to rise to their own full potential. A highly competitive economy creates jobs, generates exports, and provides more wealth and security for its members.

The competitive spirit is nurtured by attitudes and practices that have already been discussed in previous sections:

- Dissatisfaction with the status quo, always
- Direct connection to the market place
- The truth, the factual truth about clients, products, competitors, and ourselves
- The best idea wins, always
- A passion for winning, the stamina to stay the course

A case example of competitive spirit was a client who supplied the construction and home-renovation industries (very traditional sectors). It was a distant number two to the industry leader, a large company exploiting current success by repeating the same strategy from one year to the next.

Our client used continuous improvement as the core discipline to reinvent itself. Kaizen interventions were planned strategically to move the company from its current state to a far improved target state. Over time, most employees got to participate in numerous kaizen events. Regular surveys showed that this strategy has contributed to significantly increased levels of trust, commitment, and collaboration from all employees. There has been a succession of three CEOs over the period, and all have maintained the focus. The company has now been at it for ten years, getting better and stronger every year.

The results? Consistent and significant productivity gains, well above the industry average. Margins have increased while holding the line on selling prices. This has led to increased market share against a competitor who could not hold the price line. Even more importantly, the company gained the capacity to open new distribution channels and to do it with far superior reliability and just-in-time performance. Over ten years, a fivefold increase in sales and profits was attained. This, moreover, in an industry with a growth rate driven by the gross national product.

4.5   A High Performance Strategy Process

This is the heart of the solution we propose for the problem we are addressing: providing much better strategic answers to small and mid-size companies.

It consists in a different approach and a basic set of four methodologies that support this approach.

The currently dominant approach and methodologies for the formulation of strategic plans is based on a lot of effort dedicated to bottom-up analytics. This may help large corporations, but it provides little help to mid-tier companies and even in large corporations heavy analytics often tend to evolve into bureaucratic processes where there is little room for creative strategic thinking.

The approach we propose is to start from the genius inside. It is based on the observation that 60 to 80% of the information required to do strategic thinking is already in the knowledge and experience of the people inside the company.

This is usually quite sufficient to formulate strategy. No one, even in the largest corporations, expects to have 100% of the required information to take decisions, this would be a path to extinction in an ever changing world.

The challenge is to organize the information already inside the company into a strategic format. Understandably, it is naturally organized in an operational format which is required to manage day-to-day.

This is where specifically designed methodologies come into play. There are four of them which will be described below. Most of the time, they are sufficient and in such cases a company gets significant strategic insight with high effectiveness in terms of time and cost. This is the **basic process**.

Of course, there are occasions where original research and analysis are required. For many reasons, the management team may not know enough about a key subject. Then by all means do the research. But under our approach, it will likely be very focused which usually means higher quality and higher impact. This will be our second level in the process, **complements** and **additions**.

The Basic Process aims to provide a company with the strategy insights required to win today to create a better future.

Thus, the definition of strategic planning success is to arrive at decisions that will create the company's future at three levels:

- Level 1 – **Alignment** of resources to opportunities; setting and achieving stretch targets for growth and internal performance in the current business model
- Level 2 – **Incremental innovation** in and around the current business model
- Level 3 – **Radical innovation**, new space, new rules resulting in a new business model

Can all these results be achieved in a single strategic planning cycle? Hardly. Each of these strategic levels requires a specific thinking process. In terms of organizational learning, it is far more effective to build from one step to the next, possibly over a three-year timeframe.

In this view, Level 1 – Alignment is a first step in a long series of efforts to define, refine, and implement the next big idea. At this level the following questions should be answered:

- What happens if current policies and strategies are maintained (baseline forecast)?
- What are the possible future scenarios?
- What can we be best at?
- What is **the** "opportunity"?
- What are the leaders passionate about?

This can be achieved in companies where the CEO is the Chief Strategy Officer; where the rules of the game are clear and where the planning team is balanced between experience and creativity. Outside consultants can help to manage the process and lead workshops. They should provide radical thinking, and protect the team from sacred cows.

So what is the process methodology to do this? First, here is the disclaimer. Methodologies are important, they help to reduce wasted efforts, if they are good, they are based on well demonstrated practices and know how. But each situation is unique, and you have to think it through, always check your premises; cookie cutters are good for cookies, but not so much for strategy. Generic methodologies need to be adapted to each unique situation.

In our practice, we organize the project and then proceed in four steps as illustrated in Figure 4.1.

1. **Create a fact base** which involves first, project organization where we identify "what we know" and "what we don't know." This is done through the "brown box" exercise, which allows the consulting team to rapidly absorb the contents of documented past initiatives inside the company. This leads to more targeted project activities and better aligned project participant selection. Second, a Questionnaire survey: the High Performance Assessment™ (HPA). This is an anonymous questionnaire survey. It can be applied to a group of fifteen to thirty participants. It provides a strong base for future steps because it covers enterprise level issues

through one hundred questions, quantitative and qualitative, on fifteen performance dimensions. The HPA also addresses the organization's emerging strategic challenge. The final questionnaire question addresses "low-hanging fruit" and often provides highly profitable targets for immediate improvement. The High Performance Assessment™ is a well tested methodology that we have applied more than one hundred times. A well designed questionnaire survey is where operational knowledge is reorganized into strategic maps that lead to the identification of the most important strategic opportunities and issues at a given point in time.

2. **Opportunities, Goals, Strategies** addresses both "the first curve" and "the second curve". This is where creative strategic thinking is required. It will produce a framework to discuss a limited number (three to five) of opportunities and issues and making the required decisions. This is done through one or more workshops that are organized as "Innovation Lab™" a methodology discussed in more detail in Section 6.6.

3. **Operationalization** involves formatting the above decisions as business initiatives organized as a strategic or "President's" agenda (see Section 7.4). This establishes a loading, i.e. no more than three to five initiatives at a time to be executed at a predetermined pace, say quarterly for example.

4. **Follow-up** is the key to getting it done. The follow-up discipline can be provided by a Management Forum where project leaders report on completed initiatives and the next wave is reviewed and programmed (please see Section 7.3).

From time to time, this basic process will need to be enhanced by **complements** and **additions** to address a commonly identified need. This often deals with outside-in research of industry trends, market dynamics, competitor capabilities. There can also be issues and changes that require specific preparation, for example:

- **External models of excellence** provide a necessary reality check. They address the "can't be done here" and "not invented here" syndromes. The idea is to choose two or three examples of outstanding performers who can provide insight into our own situation. This selection process already helps to understand the management team's current frame of reference. One question in the High Performance Assessment asks participants for their suggestion on who they see as external models of excellence. The main value of the exercise is for everyone to gain an understanding not only of best practices at best companies but, even more importantly, of the principles and values that guide their management action.

- **Shareholders** expectations are explored through individual interviews with each stakeholder. This can then be discussed in a workshop where a higher level of objectivity can be achieved.

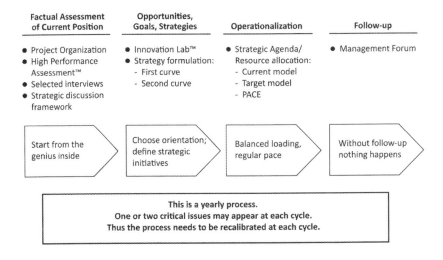

Figure 4.1. Strategic planning process template.

4.6   The Mind of the Strategist

There always comes a time during strategic planning projects when participants need to be selected. "Who?" asks the client. First, the strategic thinkers, we reply. Invariably, the clients know who are the strategic thinkers among their team. Typically, they stand out, they are different, they are the ones that ask "Why are we doing it this way? What about this other way?"

Some people will be naturally more at ease than others with strategic thinking, but it is an ability that can be nurtured in many people, if they set their mind to it.

First, strategic thinkers are **curious** about their subject; they study it all the time. Conceptual schemes, success stories, and failure stories constitute a wealth of resources in their minds of references and cross-references. They also have other interests that are not directly related—such as arts, philosophy, cooking, and sports—that expand their reference base and allow them to cross ideas from one area to the profit of another.

The second attribute is **abstract thinking**. This is the capacity to take a multitude of facts and synthesize them down to a few fundamental conclusions. This is how all the analysis becomes strategic: it is the five "whys?" and the "so what?" statement.

Third is **creativity and insight**. Napoleon Bonaparte provides the following example. Two first-class professional armies, under two highly trained generals, have been fighting it out all day. No one has yet gained an advantage. Then, at one point, very quickly, one of the armies scores a breakthrough and wins the day. One of the generals has found the weakness that became his opportunity.

Finally there is **entrepreneurship**, the capacity to break the rules and invent new ones. This is often described as "**creative destruction**" but most often, it is actually "**creative innovation**". Peter Drucker discusses entrepreneurship as follows:

> Classical economics optimizes what already exists, as does mainstream economic theory to this day (Keynes, Friedman, supply-siders). It focuses on getting the most out of existing resources and aims at establishing equilibrium...
>
> However, "the entrepreneur upsets and disorganizes"...
>
> Innovation is the specific tool of entrepreneurs...
>
> Entrepreneurship rests on a hypothesis of economy and society. The theory sees change as normal and indeed healthy. And it sees the major task in society—and

especially in the economy—as doing something different rather than doing better what is already being done…

Anyone who can face up to decision-making can learn to be an entrepreneur and to behave entrepreneurially. Entrepreneurship, then, is behavior rather than a personality trait. And its foundation lies in concept and theory rather than intuition…

Entrepreneurs see change as the norm and as healthy. Usually, they do not bring about the change themselves. But—and this defines entrepreneur and entrepreneurship—the entrepreneur always searches for change, responds to it, and exploits it as an opportunity…

Entrepreneurship is less risky than optimization in areas where the proper and profitable course is innovation…

We cannot yet develop a **theory** of innovation. But we know enough to develop, though still only in outline form, the **practice** of innovation…

4.7   The Role and Place of Consultants

Consultants are the mediators of a highly effective strategy process. They can come from inside or outside the company.

They can provide significant value on the following dimensions:

- Managing the process effectively in a timely manner.
- Providing the required documentation at each step in the process.
- Providing workshop animation which allows the CEO and his team to concentrate on brainstorming and creating strategy.
- Through individual interviews and coordination amongst the participants the consultant can mediate conflicting points of view towards a positive outcome. In a creative process, conflict is most likely, if it is well managed, it will be creative.
- The consultant should finally be the guardian of a factual, insightful discussion. Factual means truthful i.e. the facts,

only the facts. Insightful means that sacred cows, paradigms and orthodoxies are left at the door. It is only when statements such as "this is the way it is in our industry..." are set a side, that a group has a real chance to find new insights.

In order to provide this value, the consultant needs to be a strategic thinker, a good listener, an integrator, a mediator, an animator. He needs to master the tools that help leverage the genius inside the company; the methodologies to organize day-to-day operational know how into a strategic framework.

As indicated above, this can be done by one of the company's own employees. But most often, especially in small and mid-size organizations, an outsider who specializes in strategy consulting will provide more mastery of the process and greater objectivity. Usually, it is relatively easier to mediate and "push" on issues when one does not have to spend the rest of the year managing day-to-day operations.

4.8   The Emerson Electric Example

Emerson Electric is an outstanding example of what superior follow-up and disciplined execution can achieve. Their consistency is awe inspiring. For over fifty years, from 1956 to 2006, the trend in revenues and earnings per share was consistent, and the performance made Emerson a top performer year after year.

There were a few difficult years around 2000, when revenues and earnings per share actually decreased against the historical trend line. This was caused by major changes in the company's technological foundations. But as the *Economist* magazine pointed out at the time, it was almost a foregone conclusion that such a disciplined company would work its way successfully out of this challenge. And indeed, as Emerson's 2006 annual report clearly shows, they have overcome their challenges and have completely reestablished themselves on their historical trend line.

Is there a big secret here? Well, actually, yes and no. As Charles F. Knight, the company's CEO for more than twenty-five years, puts it, the Emerson processes for planning, continuous improvement, and strategic human resources are well known. The difference at Emerson is that they obviously act on these policies with great discipline and consistency.

The main elements of these processes can be summarized as follows:

- **Goals and objectives** are set to reflect the potential from markets and business strategies, but this bottom-up logic must lead to the achievement of superior levels of performance as determined from the top down, by senior management— sales growth of 15 percent, for example.
- The purpose of **strategic planning** is to define the specific initiatives that will ensure each unit meets the stretch target.
- Sales growth must be supported by continuous cost improvement. Emerson calls this its **best-cost strategy**, and the performance indicator here is 7 percent per year. This is achieved through total quality and customer satisfaction, competitive analysis, focused manufacturing, employee communication, formalized cost-reduction programs, and support of capital expenditures.
- **Organization development** is driven by **effective communications**. Every Emerson employee is able to answer four questions about his or her job: (i) What cost reductions are you working on? (ii) Who is the competition? (iii) Have you met with management in the last six months? (iv) Do you understand the economics of your job? Employees are regularly surveyed about their satisfaction on the job and leadership talent is carefully identified and nurtured.

These are coherent policies that are or should be on the books of any well-managed company. As Charles Knight says, the difference is to actually act on these policies. Some of the ways that this takes place involve considering that **not meeting an objective**, once it has been set, **is unacceptable**. To this effect, Emerson uses an **"A-B-C" budgeting process**. The "A" budget presents targeted performance for revenues, costs, and profit. The "B" budget presents a scenario with the same profit target, even if revenue targets fall short. The "C" budget provides an orderly retrenchment scenario if conditions get really bad. This forces managers to explain how profits will be maintained even under adverse market conditions. Similarly, cost-reductions targets need to be explained for at least 80 percent before the year starts. Finally, if employee surveys start trending downwards, senior leaders call immediately and expect a very clear explanation.

Superior performance at Emerson is based on grinding it out one yard at a time, day after day. Here is Charles Knight in his own words:

> In my view, the job of management is to identify and successfully implement business investment opportunities that permit us to achieve the financial targets we set.
>
> Simply put, what makes us "tick" at Emerson is an effective management process. We believe we can shape our future through careful planning and strong follow-up. Our managers plan for improved results and execute to get them. Driving this process is a set of shared values, including involvement, intensity, discipline, and persistence. We adhere to few policies or techniques that could be called unique or even unusual. But we do act on our policies, and that may indeed make us unusual.
>
> We believe, for example, that profitability is a state of mind. Experience tells us that if management concentrates on the fundamentals and consistently follows up, there is no reason why we can't achieve profits year after year—even in manufacturing businesses that many observers consider mature and unglamorous. We also believe that companies fail primarily for non analytical reasons: management knows what to do but, for some reasons, doesn't do it. That is why Emerson has a strong action orientation; we see to it that our strategies get implemented properly.
>
> A third belief is that the "long term" consists of a sequence of "short terms." Poor performance in the short term makes it more difficult to achieve strong performance in the long term. The basis of management is management from minute to minute, day to day, week to week.

Finally, it is crucial to "keep it simple." A corporation has to work hard to have a simple plan, simple communications, simple programs, and simple organizations. It takes real discipline to keep things simple.

The driving force behind all that change (at Emerson) is a simple management process that emphasizes setting targets, planning carefully, and following up closely. The process is supported by a long-standing history of continuous cost reduction and open communication and is fueled by annual dynamic planning and control cycles. Finally, it is nourished by strongly reinforced cultural values and an approach to organizational planning that is as rigorous as our approach to business planning. It is an environment in which people at all levels can and do make a difference.

Chapter 5: Incremental Innovation

"I have found thousands of ways not to do a light bulb."
—Thomas Edison

5.1   Chance Comes to Those Who Are Prepared

Louis Pasteur said that luck comes to those who are prepared. In terms of innovation, this means that new ideas and brilliant perceptions will tend to occur within a business as long as that business pursues them systematically, and with discipline. Those who do their homework can usually be found at the top of the class.

Over the medium term, innovation is your company's only hope of survival and over the shorter term, you need innovation, because:

- Innovation, not productivity, is the driver of growth.
- If you are not number one or number two in your markets, innovation is the attacker's edge to help you to get there.
- If you are number one or number two, continuous innovation is the required defense strategy: leave no gap for the attacker to exploit!

Sooner or later in any discussion on innovation, someone will make the point that according to all studies, the actual success rate is very low. So what?

- Pareto's 80/20 rule seems to apply to innovation.[2]
- If all one must really concentrate on is the 20 percent of success, what does that mean for the organization? You need to look at this as a venture capitalist, not as an accountant (at

---

[2]   Pareto's law states that in most situations, one gets 80% of the result from 20% of the effort.

least those accountants that focus only on costs and do not understand the logic of investment).

- Of course, you must have in place a process to make sure that the failures are as inexpensive as possible and provide as much learning as possible.

The purpose of the "innovation pipeline" is to transform "luck" into a profitable, predictable business process. Robert Cooper proposes crucial factors for success in product innovation, in summary:

- Doing lots of research on the consumer
- Having a structured process and exacting criteria for analysis
- Creating a really differentiated product aligned to customer needs
- Working with "best in the world" as a benchmark
- Getting top management endorsement
- Launching with adequate resources to the most receptive target markets.

A model for the innovation pipeline process is illustrated in figure 5.1. The first three steps are critical.

First, the **framework**. A clear framework directly supports at least two conditions of success.

- It will focus efforts on areas where the company wants to innovate. It will thus eliminate out-of-focus initiatives at the source.
- It will help to get support from top management. Formulating the framework should be a key part of the company's strategy. Because the CEO is the architect of this, the innovation process actually addresses his strategy.

Thus a clear framework should address the following:

- **The innovation objective**. This creates motivation and provides a measure for success. Some companies use a replacement rule, such as 20 percent of sales per year from new products. Others use competitive benchmarks such as "recognized as the most innovative." The key is to propose a stretch target.

- **The innovation strategy**. Is it to be the technology leader or follower, low or high budget, or a balance?
- **The target scope or area for innovation.** Which customer groups, what applications, and which technologies are we targeting?
- **The responsibility for innovation**. Is there at least one person who can be contacted by people who have suggestions?
- **The resources for innovation.** Access to networks (e.g., Procter & Gamble's "Connect and Develop"), staffing, funding.
- **The culture for innovation.** Is the organization characterized by a market-driven entrepreneurial business philosophy, the capacity to see and act on opportunities, a structure that provides space for new initiatives, management systems that react quickly, understanding, and managing innovation as a venture capital portfolio and people policies that encourage and reward risk taking?

Clearly, becoming an innovation-driven organization requires much learning by trial and error and constant and consistent communication of the desired culture.

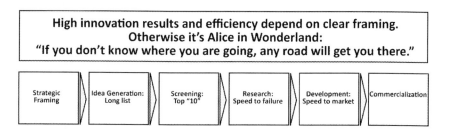

Figure 5.1. The innovation pipeline.

5.2　Idea Creation, Customer Involvement

Incremental innovation completes the alignment strategy by providing an important element to achieve above average growth. Incremental innovation also prepares the ground for radical innovation by developing the capacity to create ideas and the willingness to take risks.

Two questions can be asked about idea creation: Which ideas work better and how do you produce them?

A study in 1999[3] concluded that the 111 successful new products out of 200 that were studied had the following profile:

- Moderately new to the market
- Based on tried-and-tested technology
- Saved money, met customer needs, and supported existing behaviors.

The authors go on to categorize ideas according to their source and propose that some sources are much more successful than others. "Need spotting," "solution spotting," market research and random events are highly successful sources, whereas "mental inventions" and "trend following" are much less so (i.e., start from a real consumer need!).

There are jobs in an organization that are specifically dedicated to finding ideas, for example in R&D and marketing. But in reality, anyone can play. It is a question of finding an interesting problem and then dedicating oneself to solving it. James Webb Young had a career in advertising in which he came up with breakthrough ideas time after time. When he retired, someone asked him how he had done it. This is how he described his technique.

There is a practical technique for creating ideas. It involves principles and a method:

- The first principle is that an idea is nothing more nor less than a new combination of old elements.

---

[3]　Jacob Goldenberg, Donald Leherman, and David Magursky, Marketing Science Institute, 1999.

- The second principle is that the capacity to bring old elements into new combinations depends largely on the ability to see relationships.
- The method to produce ideas is as follows:
    1. The gathering of raw materials—both the material of your immediate problem and the materials which come from a constant enrichment of your store of general knowledge
    2. The working over of these materials in your mind
    3. The incubating stage, where you let something beside the conscious mind do the work of synthesis
    4. The actual birth of the Idea—the "Eureka! I have it!" stage
    5. The final shaping and development of the idea to the practical usefulness.

You will find in figure 5.2 a list of twenty five steps towards generating new product ideas.

1. Establish a focal point in the company—an idea person
2. Identify the possible sources of new-product ideas
3. Use focus groups of customers or potential users to generate new-product ideas
4. Set up a user panel that meets periodically to discuss problems or needs that might lead to new-product ideas
5. Survey your customers
6. Observe your customers as they use your product
7. Install a customer hot line
8. Maximize your sales and service staff access to and interaction with innovative users
9. Hire sales and technical people who can recognize potential new products
10. Promote your quest for new products to users by targeting likely innovators, defining the product desired, and providing a reward
11. Routinely survey your competition
12. Organize a trade-show visitation program
13. Set up a clipping service for domestic and foreign trader publications
14. Examine patent files and the *Official Gazette* regularly
15. Use idea brokers and product-license brokers
16. Attend product-licensing shows
17. Visit your suppliers' labs and spend time with their technical people
18. Set up a system to handle ideas submitted by private inventors in a legally sound fashion
19. Visit key universities and researchers. Consider putting several key researchers on a retainer
20. Set up a new-product idea suggestion scheme in your company
21. Run a new-product idea contest complete with publicity and prizes for the best ideas
22. Run several brainstorming sessions using in-house and outside people. Use the format described in this chapter
23. Run a new-product contest targeted specifically at sales and technical people

24. Establish lines of communication to the sales force. Use a new-product-opportunity call report, a telephone hot line, a reminding decal, and presentations at sales meetings
25. Organize creativity sessions involving sales and technical people in the same session.

Figure 5.2. Twenty-five steps toward generating new-product ideas.

Source: Robert G. Cooper, *Winning at New Products* (Massachusetts: Addison Wesley Publishing, 1986).

5.3   Screening and Testing: Speed to Failure

We learn through failure.

This is how science proceeds. A theory is seen as valid because it explains a certain set of phenomena. Then a new theory replaces it because it explains more or better, or in some cases differently. Some theories actually live side by side and serve specific and different purposes, Newton's physics and quantum mechanics, for example. Similarly, a company needs both disciplined methodologies and radical thinking. Before getting to a successful new theory, scientists will test and discard a vast number of hypotheses. How? By following and respecting the scientific method, which is deceptively simple:

- Here is a proposed hypothesis or new idea.
- Here is a test to validate it or not.
- Here are the results.
- If yes, move forward.
- If no, start again.

The same is true for innovation in business. There should be no conflict between supporting the creation of as many ideas as possible and the required screening and testing down to the few limited theories that warrant further effort.

There can be a lot of hand wringing around this. Should we be scared that we will destroy creativity with a high kill rate? No, if the attitude is correct, there is no real risk there. In any case, moving too many ideas forward will prove quickly unprofitable and eventually destroy senior management support.

The other danger is "falling in love." Just because someone thinks that something is great doesn't mean that it is. Figure 5.3 presents a long and excellent list of fifty questions which should help to weed out the weaker ideas.

---

1. What problem does the innovation solve?
2. Do people perceive it as a problem?
   - How do you know?
3. If not, at what point would it become a problem for them?
4. What was the source of the idea?
   - Finding an answer to a problem
   - Finding a new use for an existing technology
   - It came out of market research
   - It's following a trend
   - You just dreamed it up.
5. Does the innovation fulfill a previously unmet need?
6. What new possibilities might it open up?
7. How do you improve your chances at the following stages of the adoption decision process?
   - Knowledge that the innovation exists
   - Recognition that it solves a problem
   - Influencing the adopter's decision (they may be researching it)
   - The decision process itself (normally buying)
   - Implementation
   - Retention and confirmation.
8. Describe a typical early adopter. What will they want from the innovation?
9. Describe a typical late majority adopter. What will they want from the innovation?
10. How must the innovation change to move from the early adopters to the late majority?
11. Who or what will influence each group of adopters?
12. What is the old way of doing things?

---

13. What will adopters perceive as the relative advantage of the innovation?
14. Is it compatible with their values, experiences, culture?
15. Will users find it easy to understand?
16. Can people easily try out the innovation before committing themselves?
17. Can they observe its performance before they use it?
18. Are there risks associated with using the innovation, or does it reduce some kind of risk?
19. Does it deny people the ability to make important choices of their own?
20. Does the innovation harm or enhance the user's image?
21. Can it do the job sufficiently? If so, how?
22. How different is the innovation from things with which people might have had a good or bad experience?
23. What are the costs of adopting or switching, both in time and money?
24. What is the cost benefit to the user?
25. Does the innovation tap into any network effects?
26. Is it interoperable with rival or complementary products?
27. Is it dependent on any other innovations in order to work effectively?
28. Does the innovation create or challenge a standard?
29. Can it be built and maintained easily and cheaply?
30. Is disposal easy and cheap?
31. What inducements or subsidies exist to promote the innovation?
32. Which of these characteristics (points 14-31) will be most important to early adopters?
33. Which will be most important to the late majority?
34. Which characteristics are you, the innovator, actively promoting?
35. Is there a difference? If so, should you be worried?
36. What is the innovation's underlying Behavioural Premise?
37. What environmental clues are there?

38. In what way is the innovation different from what you see in those environmental clues?
39. What social or economic forces will drive people to adopt the innovation?
40. Will you overcome the following nebulous resistance factors:
    - "I can't be bothered"
    - "It's too fiddly"
    - "I'm OK as I am"
41. Has the innovation been the subject of excessive hype?
42. What do market forecasters predict?
43. Do you believe them? If so, why?
44. Ask someone to tell you if you show any signs of the following:
    - Projecting your own needs on to users
    - Excessive overconfidence
    - Symptoms of groupthink
    - Refusal to accept feedback or ignoring negative results from research.
45. By what criteria will you judge success?
    - Market share
    - Technical excellence
    - Customer satisfaction
    - Return on investment
    - Competitive advantage
46. In what time frame and in what context?
47. Do you have a structured process with clearly defined criteria for Stop/Go decisions?
48. How will you sell the innovation? By promoting features or asking questions?
49. What would you do if market research showed no demand for your innovation?
50. At what point would you give up?

Figure 5.3. Screening and testing checklist.
Source: Franklin Carl, *Why Innovation Fails* (London: Spiro Press, 2003).

5.4   Organizing and Managing Incremental Innovation

Innovation, and more precisely, **continuous incremental innovation**, happens when supportive organization and processes are in place: it is a mentality and a system.

There are conditions that support incremental innovation:

- Analyze systematically all sources for innovative opportunity.
- Use both sides of the brain: rationality and creativity.
- Keep it simple and focused.
- Start small: a little bit of money, a few people, and a limited target market.
- But aim big: leadership at maturity.

Inversely, some attitudes and practices will destroy innovation:

- Doing too many things at once.
- Mixing managerial and innovative activities.
- Creating mistrust: mutual criticism, detailed accounting of every detail, long approval processes, bosses that know everything.

When developing the capacity for innovation, one good thing leads to another. The very same high-performance, high-commitment organization practices that are the foundation of the alignment strategy are also the essential foundations of continuous innovation. The qualities of trust, collaboration, and widespread participation found in a high-commitment organization also constitute the fertile ground in which an effective innovation process can grow.

Finally, there is the question of who can do this? Are innovators and entrepreneurs a special breed? No. Entrepreneurship is a question of behavior, policies, and practices rather than personality. For example, look at the growing number of older large-corporation managers in the United States who make entrepreneurship their second career.

In successful entrepreneurial businesses, nobody seems to worry whether a given person is likely to do a good job of development or not. People of all temperaments and backgrounds apparently do equally well.

By and large, people who do not feel comfortable as innovators or as entrepreneurs will not volunteer for such jobs, so the gross misfits eliminate themselves. The rest can learn the practices of innovation. Executives who have performed well in other assignments will generally do a decent job as entrepreneurs. The large body of literature on the "entrepreneurial personality" furthers a pointless discussion.

The following questions should help to test your organization's current innovation capacity.

- Is innovation a key feature in our company's mission or value statement?
- Does our CEO or chairman challenge the organization frequently to become more innovative or improve its innovation performance?
- Within our company, is innovation widely regarded as a critical competitive advantage?
- Has a senior executive been given explicit responsibility for improving our company's innovation performance?
- Does the monthly or quarterly business review process focus clearly on innovation performance (as compared with overall financial performance)?
- Does our company regularly and systematically benchmark its innovation performance against other companies?
- Does our company have awards or recognition programs tied explicitly to (non-technical) innovation?
- Can a specific individual reap a sizable financial reward for a particular instance of innovation?
- Does our company have a formal innovation process (beyond R&D and new product development) that surfaces, develops, and supports new business concepts?
- Does our culture support risk taking?

5.5   The P&G Example

Procter & Gamble got a wake-up call in 2000. By that time, its volume growth was flat and its stock had lost half of its value.

A. G. Lafley became CEO that year and saw that P&G's traditional strengths in chemical engineering and marketing would not be the drivers of future growth. He saw that his company was more oriented to product technology than to user experience, and to get new growth, it had to begin from the consumer.

Lafley turned to design innovation in order to increase top-line revenue growth. He is not alone in this quest. According to a survey of 940 senior executives by the Boston Consulting Group, increasing top-line revenues through innovation has become essential to success in their industries.

P&G's focus on continuous product innovation is based on an insightful understanding of changing consumer lifestyles. Some of the steps used by P&G are as follows:

- A vice-president for design, innovation, and strategy was appointed.
- The design staff was quadrupled, even during a major, company-wide staff reduction effort.
- Designers started working directly with research and development staff to develop new products. This changed the focus from technology to the consumer.
- New outside consultants oriented to design innovation were brought in.
- Division heads are regularly contacted to identify possible opportunities which designers might address.
- Innovation "gyms" have been established to train managers in the new design thinking.
- A design board, staffed with outsiders, has been created to provide an independent perspective on products, brand extension, and marketing.

All these moves work to change the organization culture toward innovation and to set up a process that supports this. These are necessary steps, but they are typical of any well-organized effort in most companies. What is really unique and interesting is the underlying model of open innovation that P&G calls "Connect and Develop." This is how L. Huston and N. Sakkab describe this process:

> Most companies are still clinging to what we call the invention model, centered on a bricks-and-mortar R&D infrastructure and the idea that their innovation must principally reside within their own four walls. To be sure, these companies are increasingly trying to buttress their laboring R&D departments with acquisitions, alliances, licensing, and selective innovation outsourcing. And they're launching Skunk Works, improving collaboration between marketing and R&D, tightening go-to-market criteria, and strengthening product portfolio management.
>
> But these are incremental changes, bandages on a broken model. Strong words, perhaps, but consider the facts: most mature companies have to create organic growth of 4% to 6% year in, year out. How are they going to do it? For P&G, that's the equivalent of building a $4 billion business this year alone.
>
> We discovered that important innovation was increasingly being done at small and midsize entrepreneurial companies. The internet had opened up access to talent markets throughout the world.
>
> We knew that most of P&G's best innovations had come from connection ideas across internal businesses. Betting that these connections were the key to future growth, Lafley made it our goal to acquire 50% of our innovations outside the company. The strategy wasn't to replace the capabilities of our 7,500 researchers and support staff, but to better leverage them. Half of our new products, Lafley said, would come from our own labs, and half would come through them.
>
> We needed to move the company's attitude from resistance to innovations "not invented here" to enthusiasm to those "proudly found elsewhere." And we needed to change how we defined, and perceived, our R&D organization—from

7,500 people inside to 7,500 plus 1.5 million outside, with a permeable boundary between them.

The model works. Through connect and develop—along with improvements in other aspects of innovation related to product cost, design, and marketing—our R&D productivity has increased by nearly 60%. Our innovation success rate has more than doubled, while the cost of innovation has fallen. R&D investment as a percentage of sales is down from 4.8% in 2000 to 3.4% today. And, in the last two years, we've launched more than 100 new products for which some aspect of execution came from outside the company. Five years after the company's stock collapse in 2000, we have doubled our share price and have a portfolio of 22 billion-dollar brands.

Chapter 6: Radical Innovation

"Our mission is to make a significant difference."
—Institute for Research in Immunology and Cancer, University of Montreal

6.1   Creative Destruction

The economist Joseph Schumpeter saw capitalism as a process of radical innovation created by entrepreneurs who discover significantly better ways of doing things and replace the established order: **creative destruction**.

Large corporations, often with a storied history, disappear regularly. This shows without a doubt that, as Richard Foster said, "The right of any corporation to exist is not perpetual but has to be continuously earned."

Radical innovation changes the game. It happens everywhere. So it will happen in your domain. There is only one question: Will you do it or will someone else do it to you?

Innovation is the specific tool of entrepreneurs. Through innovation, they exploit change as an opportunity for creating a new product or a new service. An **innovation** is an increase of the performance on the yield on resources; an innovation changes the value and satisfaction obtained from resources by the customer from the resources.

This chapter considers change as an opportunity for new products, services, processes, or complete business models.

For corporations, this is not a natural act. Typically, companies are built for continuity and the elimination of risk. They try to achieve predictable outcomes through control. Of course, this leads to maturity and to eventual decline; witness the Fortune 500 companies who currently stay on the list for an average of twenty years. As the pace of change increases, this tenure is bound to get even shorter. Sustainable advantages remain such only for a short period.

It is hard to overstate how big a challenge this represents for corporations that are wired for predictability through control:

- Innovation requires entrepreneurial thinking. This means deviant thinking, thinking outside the box. This runs against thinking in terms of more and better of the same, of conformity.
- Innovation requires different processes and a different policy framework.
- Innovation is organized differently.
- It is no easy task to make risk-taking and radical thinking accepted at the same time and in a place where most of the activity is dedicated to conformity.

Both very good and very bad companies fail equally to deal successfully with disruptive innovation.

Some companies don't deserve success, because they are well established but arrogant. They have become bureaucratic, management is inbred, they maximize short-term returns—they have lost the edge.

According to Christensen's research, there are also very well managed companies who fail to deal with disruptive innovation. This is because of their very strengths. They invest where their current customers have needs, whereas disruptive innovations are typically adopted by small niche markets that do not have sufficient size, at the beginning, to be of interest to well established or larger enterprises.

Christensen concludes that the problem can only be resolved when new markets are developed around new definitions of value and when the responsibility for building such new businesses is placed in new, smaller organizations totally focused on the new business and its customers. This, again, stands in contrast to incremental innovation, which should fit perfectly well within the current organization.

Richard Foster, quoted below, makes the point that as the attacker and the innovator, the entrepreneur is bound to be the eventual winner.

Entrepreneurs know change is ongoing; they believe that they can create it and profit from it. They are ready to deal with the risks and the necessary failures involved in innovation and change. Most of all, they understand that complete and limited focus on the status quo is the highest-risk strategy.

Foster uses the "S" curve as his model. The S curve plots the level of effort and the performance produced. At the bottom, there is much start-up effort and little result. Then, there is breakthrough and rapid growth as the innovation is adopted in the marketplace and replaces the incumbents. Finally, there is maturity as the innovation reaches its full potential and further investment produces diminishing returns. The innovator has become the defender. The logic of creative destruction is that he or someone else is bound to start the cycle all over again. It all depends on the mindset.

> In the end, *Innovation: The Attacker's Advantage* came to be about companies that have more up years than their competitors because they recognize that they must be close to ruthless in cannibalizing their current products and processes just when they are most lucrative, and begin the search again, over and over. It is about the inexorable and yet stealthy challenge of new technology and the economics of substitution which force companies to behave like the mythical phoenix, a bird that periodically crashed to earth in order to rejuvenate itself. It is thus not a book about process—seven steps to new products—but instead about a point of view about business in which change, success and failure seem to come more and more rapidly.
>
> Henry Ford, long ago, understood the message of this book. In *My Life and Work*, he wrote, "If to petrify is success, all one has to do is to humor the lazy side of the mind; but if to grow is success, then one must wake up anew every morning and keep awake all day. I saw great businesses become but the ghost of a name because someone thought they could be managed just as they were always managed, and though the management may have been most excellent in its day, its excellence consisted in its alertness to its day, and not in slavish following of its yesterdays. Life, as I see it, is not a location, but a journey. Even the man who most feels himself 'settled' is not settled—he is probably sagging back. Everything is in

flux, and was meant to be. Life flows. We may live at the same number of the street, but it is never the same man who lives there." And later in the same book: "It could almost be written down as a formula that when a man begins to think that he at last has found his method, he had better begin a most searching examination of himself to see whether some part of his brain has not gone to sleep."[4]

6.2   To Make a Significant Difference

An organization (or an individual) has had high impact when its peers recognize that it has made a significant difference.

This is the essence of **strategic intent**; there is an overarching goal whose achievement is not directly evident from the current situation. The gap is wide, very wide, but achieving the goal would make a significant difference to clients and the industry. Imagination and hard work will be required. Risks will be involved. The rewards, of course, will be commensurate.

The mission of the people who work at IRIC (the Immunology and Cancer Research Institute at the Université de Montréal) is to cure cancer, or at least a few of its types. They have put in place research processes and collaborative work models that are quite different from traditional approaches. They attract the best of the best students. The IRIC is a new type of organization in its domain; it still has to make its significant contribution, but the goal is clear, the processes are in place, it is attracting the best resources, and it is achieving a remarkable success rate with funding sources.

Another example is Soichiro Honda. Just after World War II, he was repairing motors in Tokyo with very limited means. Yet, in his mind, he was going to be the next Henry Ford.

This is not for everyone. Five percent of the people who get brain cancer survive. Why? Because they invent a new life, immediately, radically. They change the goal, they change the means.

Creating a new model that establishes new rules, and subsequently

---

[4]   Richard N. Foster, *Innovation: The Attacker's Advantage* (New York: Summit, 1986), pages 21-22.

executing it with excellence through a high-commitment organization is a tall order.

The Cirque du Soleil is often cited as an example of the invention of new rules and new market space. And indeed, the Cirque du Soleil has reinvented the traditional circus industry. It has done this by effectively considering the world to be its stage—its projects are financed by its partners, and it firmly remains a private company ("Creativity before cash," as they put it).

Radical business model, radical market definition, radical financing; a company that effectively creates a new future. But the Cirque du Soleil is a startup. It was created this way in order to solve some very practical problems (i.e., animals are expensive; replace them with humans). Creating an equivalent, radical change in an existing and already very successful enterprise is a more complex challenge. It requires management leadership equally capable of entrepreneurial creative destruction and the management of operational excellence— to make incremental and radical thinkers collaborate successfully at the same time, in the same place. It also needs to set high standards and, typically, to raise organizational culture from average to high commitment. This requires teaching by example.

Setting goals that will result in making a significant difference requires vision and courage. It is so much easier to optimize the status quo. As in any endeavor, it is a question of how one chooses to see a problem.

Here is a client example that illustrates how a core competency, or technology, was first leveraged incorrectly with disastrous results and then used effectively with stellar results.

This client was an engineering-construction firm of more than three thousand professionals. Understandably, it wanted to diversify and expand outside its contract-driven, win-lose, traditional business. To that end, it undertook a number of small acquisitions of startups in businesses, which required leveraging its strong base of engineering/ technology talent. This worked out very well, and soon the firm had a portfolio of more than twenty ventures.

The seed of disaster consisted in the company's ignorance of the inherent limits of its core competency: **project management**. The engineers were indeed excellent at moving a venture from idea to operational company, but operational companies need industry-specific expertise at the top. This can never be substituted by project management, however good you are at it.

This is a typical blind spot that one encounters in professional firms. To accountants, accounting skills can deal with any problem, to lawyers, legal skills, and so on. If all you have is a hammer, all problems tend to look like nails.

For this client, far too many ventures failed. The firm bled money. The CEO was replaced. Our work with the new CEO required fast, high-impact results. A fact-driven diagnostic identified more than twenty-five areas for immediate improvement. Our role was to manage the close-order execution of these projects, to be project managers in the turnaround of this firm of project managers! Sometimes an external perspective is required, even when dealing with your core competency.

Most of the venture portfolio was liquidated. The firm then concentrated on three business sectors that clearly fit its core competency. It has since seen a stellar performance.

6.3   Growth Platforms

Growth platforms are product innovation raised to a higher level. Typically, product innovation will happen in the context of the current business, in the course of current operations; it is incremental. Platforms are at enterprise level; they create new business domains. Their impact is far greater; therefore, they are radical innovations.

Eventually, even companies with superior growth histories run out of steam. Their industry matures, and their past innovations achieve full participation of their target markets.

So then, how can we meet growth expectations from financial markets and boards of directors that in time become significantly higher than what organic growth from the current business will provide?

Major **acquisitions** represent a high-risk answer. Numerous studies have concluded that 50 percent or more of acquisitions have destroyed value.

Acquisitions can provide speed as well as good returns when a company has a clear and high-performing business model that is replicable through geographic and/or market expansion. Or when there are smaller, high-fit businesses available for acquisition. Such situations present a firm that has the financial capacity to consolidate within its sectors, with the opportunity to gain a lot of speed profitably. There are two keys to success in such a strategy:

- The criteria used to select an acquisition must be clear and applied with discipline.
- There must be an equally clear and "non-negotiable" acquisition integration framework. For the acquiring company, this precludes the internal dilution of their high performing model, and, for the acquiree, it provides incoming staff with clear indicators of how to work and grow in their new workplace.

Acquisitions that do not fit a high-value creation model are much more difficult to justify. Often, these situations involve much larger acquisition/merger targets. A first barrier is the bidding process created by the seller. The winner in this process will have the most optimistic estimate of the potential gains of the acquisition. This typically leaves little room for the difficulties and shortfalls that are bound to occur during integration.

The second difficulty in such "mergers of equals" lies in the approach to integration. Should each company retain its own management model? Should the "best of each" be combined into a new model? Should the acquirer impose its model?

The first option begs the question of where the benefits will come from. The second takes a lot of time; thus, it also reduces the benefits. The third option fits into our proposed acquisition model—*if* the acquirer brings a superior management policy to the transaction, thus creating superior value by applying it to new operations.

An acquisition model based on hard value creation criteria will tend to limit the scope of acquisitions in a firm. Thus, much of the growth will have to be driven by innovation, that is, by "bringing something new to the party."

"New Growth Platforms" as they are described by Laurie, Doz, and Sheer provide a valid direction to find and exploit major growth opportunities.

The key characteristic is that such new growth platforms, or what IBM calls "emerging business initiatives" (see section 6.7), are enterprise-level projects reporting directly to the CEO. Their nature is to create a new game or fundamentally change the current game.

For example, when UPS saw that its core small parcel delivery business was maturing, it explored client needs that could be met with its existing skills. In time, the Service Parts Logistics (SPL) unit was created and developed a leadership position in a new domain with a $6 billion potential of profitable revenues per year.

Laurie, Doz, and Sheer define growth platforms as the space for opportunity created by the common interface of three sets of variables:

- The company's current and evolving capabilities
- Unmet or latent customer needs
- Forces of change in the broader environment, such as technologies, regulations, and social trends

To exploit such opportunities, more than a single new product is required. Often, a whole new business is required. The scale is strategic, it challenges conventional wisdom, and the means are different: independence from current business protocols, positioning at the most senior level, significant CEO environment. In their research of companies successful at creating new growth platforms, Laurie, Doz, and Sheer found a high degree of consistency in how such companies approach the challenge:

1. They put a highly credible growth officer in charge, often a candidate to be the next CEO.
2. They put the team ahead of the idea. An empowered team with resources and decision-making authority will create new ideas, not the other way around.
3. The positioning of a new growth platform team respects the "somewhat in/somewhat out" relationship to the core business that has been identified as a key requirement in

numerous studies. They are sufficiently independent to have the time horizon and the performance metrics that are specific to new ventures. They are adequately "in" to be able to tap into required resources.

4. They have the guaranteed, predictable financial independence that is required as protection from the core business performance logic and that can only be given by the CEO.

5. They follow a systematic process.

Growth platforms are enterprise-level initiatives. As such, they are under the direct responsibility of the CEO. Actual project leadership can be, and in most cases is, assigned to a senior leader with strong entrepreneurial skills.

6.4   New Market Space

The concept of new market space aims to create a new business system based on a new definition of customer benefits.

The successful creation of a new value proposition provides significant advantages, which can last for many years before competition moves in and traditional market-share wars become the center of strategic focus. As Peter Drucker once put it, the most effective strategy is to "hit them where they ain't."

The methodologies that can support the creation of new market-space strategies have been traditionally less developed than those related to competing in existing markets. W. Chan Kim and Renée Mauborgne have made a significant contribution to filling this gap in a number of *Harvard Business Review* articles, and more recently in the book *Blue Ocean Strategy*. They propose three basic analytical tools to help managers make value innovation into a systematic process instead of having to rely on a stroke of genius:

- **The Strategy Canvas** structures the analysis of competitive factors at play in a given industry and the level (high/low) that each major competitor places on each factor. Interestingly, it is often the case that the offerings of most competitors are similar and track around the same curve.

- **The Four Actions Framework** aims to identify new market space from the analysis in the strategy canvas. This is done by questioning what can be **reduced, eliminated, raised,** or **created.**
- **The Eliminate – Reduce – Raise – Create Grid** summarizes the most effective scenario identified through the previous analysis. It helps (and forces) managers to reach a balanced conclusion on the breakthrough "Blue Ocean Strategy."

These three methodologies are illustrated in figure 6.1.

Creating new market space, "Blue Ocean Strategy" as Kim and Mauborgne call it, requires the capacity to reconstruct current industry barriers and competitor positions. This is creative thinking quite "outside the box," even radical. The authors underline that even Blue Ocean Strategies will eventually mature. There are no ideal industries or ideal companies. There are only companies with excellent management leadership who ask the questions that can change the game and create the conditions that allow it to happen.

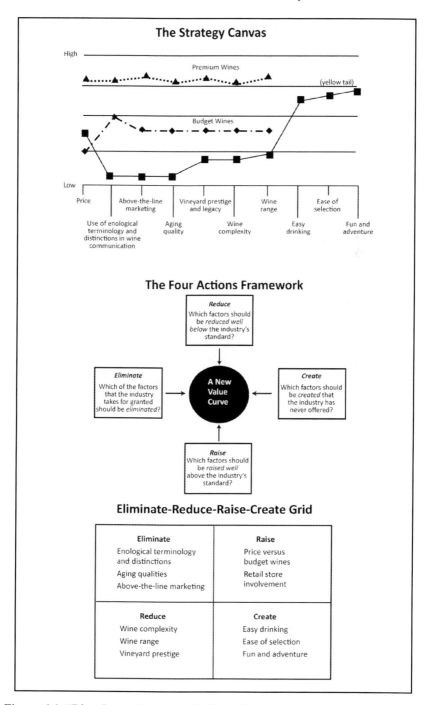

Figure 6.1. "Blue Ocean Strategy" W. Chan Kim and Renée Mauborgne, Blue Ocean Strategy, Harvard Business School Press, 2005

6.5   High Performance Work Models

Peter Drucker saw management as a disruptive innovation. To him, management is a "useful knowledge," a "*techné*," like engineering or medicine, which has allowed people to work together in organizations and created a brand new type of society (theory of the firm).

Yet, Gary Hamel argues in a recent book that at one hundred years old, it is time to reinvent management. He suggests much flatter organizations and putting most decision-making authority into the hands of the people—a significant contrast with traditional hierarchical, command-and-control models.

Actually, both command-and-control and high-performance work models, such as Hamel suggests, have been around for quite some time. Baron and Kreps provide an excellent description of the more traditional and the high-commitment people processes. Please see figure 6.2 for a summary.

The significant impact of the high-performance model has been well documented. Edward Lawler has carried out a multi-year survey of the penetration of these concepts in American enterprises. What he judges to be high-performance environments represent about 20 percent of the same and remains fairly stable. Why is this, if the benefits are so great?

Two reasons can be advanced. First, to gain the required commitment, the company has to give a lot, mostly in terms of employment guarantees. Many may think they do not have the requisite conditions to do this. Second, this requires a mindset and a type of leadership that many companies may not be willing to commit to. Please refer back to the Nucor example in section 3.6. Here is how that company's long-time leader describes their journey:

> We don't have much cynicism around Nucor. What's more, things have really changed since those dark days of 1982. We have prospered in an industry where many others have struggled. So we're not just unusual in terms of the commitment we've made to our people. We're unusually successful, too.
>
> What we did was push aside the notion that managers and employees have inherently separate interests. We've joined with our employees to pursue a goal we can all

believe in: long-term survival. We run Nucor first and foremost to ensure that, a decade or two from now, there will still be a place for our children and grandchildren to work without being laid off. That is our higher cause.

Don't get the wrong idea—we each have our individual ambitions, too. Our employees want to make the very best living they can. And our executives worry about profitability as much as those in any company. We're people, not zealots.

But we're people with a long-term perspective. The way we see it, making a living in today's economy is like crossing a broad and stormy sea. You could jump straight in and start swimming. Of course, that would be foolish. People with sense will get together and build themselves a boat. And when the seas get a little rough, you could run around pushing your shipmates overboard. People with composure work together to pull through the storms. They deal with the perils of the moment together, never forgetting that the people around them represent their best hope of reaching a better future.[5]

---

[5] Ken Iverson, *Plain Talk* (New York: John Wiley & Sons, 1998), pages 15, 16 & 17.

How are these goals to be accomplished? There is no single one-size-fits-all array of practices, but instead a list from which organizations pick and choose. Different authors have different master lists: ours follows:

- *Employment guarantees:* Workers will not be discharged except perhaps for grave errors of omission or commission.
- *Egalitarianism in word and deed:* Distinctions among workers at different levels of the hierarchy are aggressively deemphasized. Everyone is part of one big team. Symbolic distinctions—for instance, separate washrooms, dining facilities, and reserved parking spots for executives—are eliminated or downplayed, and real distinctions (most significantly, in compensation levels) are also deemphasized.
- Emphasis on *self-managing teams and team production.*
- *Job enlargement* (the job includes more tasks than is typical) and *enrichment* (the variety and challenge of tasks is larger than usual).
- *Premium compensation: efficiency wages and superior benefits.*
- *Incentive compensation based on team, unit, or firmwide performance.*
- *Extensive socialization and training* of employees, including cross-training.
- *Extensive job rotations.*
- *Open information* about all aspects of the enterprise.
- *Open channels of communication:* Employees at all levels are allowed and expected to contribute ideas. Associated with this—and with the downplaying of hierarchical distinctions—are flattened hierarchies.
- *A strong culture* of egalitarian teamwork, often focused on *some superordinate goal,* such as zero defects or the organization's mission and "vision."
- *Extensive screening* of prospective employees, emphasizing cultural fit.
- Strong emphasis on ownership, both symbolic and financial (through stock).

This is quite a long list, and on similar lists presented by other writers, you will find some items that we've decided to omit—for instance, some authors put internal staffing/promotion on this list. Many organizations will implement only a few of these items. But, as we shall see, the items fit together very nicely; the complementarities are strong, so that if you elect to do some of these, you are likely to want to do others as well.

Figure 6.2. *The means of high-commitment people processes.*

Source: James N. Baron and David M. Kreps, Strategic Human Resources (New York: John Wiley & Sons Inc., 1999), page 190.

6.6   Jump-Start the Process: The Innovation Lab™

The **Innovation Lab™** is a well-established and well-documented methodology (for example, by Richard Pasquale at Shell). The idea is to create a privileged space to explore and test new ideas.

The Innovation Lab™ methodology aims to turbo-charge the process of finding and executing breakthrough ideas—and to do this quickly, typically within five to eight weeks.

Most often, the Innovation Lab™ is used in established companies where the old game is over, when big answers or big gains must be achieved in a short period of time.

New models cannot be designed by ever more refined analyses of the current situation and focusing all efforts on the current paradigm. New, bold questions need to be asked. When answered successfully, they will raise the game by quantum leaps. Here are some actual client examples:

- **Winning in America**: How can a Canadian regional leader gain a significant North American position?
- **Strategic HR**: How can a traditional personnel function be transformed into a corporate strategic competitive advantage for a financial institution with ten thousand employees?
- **The "Marines"**: How can we double profits—now?
- **The "Air Force"**: How can we identify best growth opportunities to restart healthy growth, with limited funds?

- **Value added in commodity products**: How can we identify new applications, attributes, that will change the selling proposition from "pounds" to "value added products"?

Companies with a high entrepreneurial drive, where they keep looking for the next big opportunity, are an ideal setting for the Innovation Lab™.

The Innovation Lab™ is composed of two parts. The "what" (the exploration part) and the "how" (the getting-it-done part). This is illustrated in figure 6.3.

Exploration is the heart of the process. Exploration involves the willingness to suspend disbelief and to keep looking past the first good ideas. There is invariably a better one later on. Thus, the time allotted for idea creation should not be shortened. Think of it as a brainstorming exercise. Avoid asking "how" too quickly and concentrate on the "what." Dealing with "how" too early will preclude many interesting "whats" from being identified.

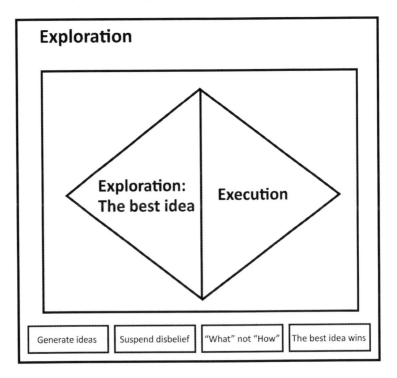

Figure 6.3. Exploration.

The second ingredient for success is selecting the team of "explorers."

A team of explorers is created from people mostly inside the company. This respects the proposition that the "genius is inside." But this is a creativity challenge, so it is important that new voices, from both inside and outside, be brought into the process. Diversity of experiences and points of view are the fundamental ingredients of creativity.

A leader needs to be appointed. Much depends on the choice of the **captain**—someone for whom there is no alternative but complete mission success.

Finally, the exploration team should be given a fairly short time to produce results: this focuses the mind. Typically, five to eight weeks elapsed time is appropriate.

The Innovation Lab™ process typically involves the following steps:

- **Definition.** Define a mandate for breakthrough innovation/ quantum results.
- **Workshop I.** At the first one-day workshop, participants will be provided with "explorer" concepts and mindsets. Then, the preparatory framework will be presented and discussed. Possible avenues will be tested and mandates will be assigned to individuals or small two-person teams. They will ask, "What is the opportunity in this space? How can we change the rules?" They will have two to four weeks to report back.
- **Workshop II.** Individuals and teams report on their discoveries, and the group first assesses each possibility individually. Then a portfolio is created. "How" issues are identified and assigned. Participants have two weeks to complete their mandate. This workshop sometimes takes place off site and provides good opportunity for extracurricular activities.
- **Workshop III.** Given a successful second phase, the proposed target model should emerge. At the end of this one-day workshop, a final draft proposal can be documented. This includes a program to get it done.

- In a way, the Innovation Lab™ is a development of the Kaizen concept at the operational level to the strategic level initiatives.

6.7   The Entrepreneur

The fundamental argument of this book is that the object of strategic planning is to create the future. This requires the identification of breakthrough opportunities that can be turned into radical innovations. Much ambiguity and risk is involved in this transformation. This is not the analysis and extrapolation of the traditional strategic planning approach. Rather, this requires entrepreneurship, which was described by Joseph Schumpeter when he co-founded such a program at the Harvard Business School as "the pursuit of opportunity without regard to the resources currently controlled."

Companies can and need to act proactively in order to foster radical innovation in three complementary ways:

- First, there cannot be radical innovation if there is not incremental innovation. This respects the fact that great leaps are hard to achieve if you have not practiced at little jumps first.
- Second, radical innovation is the work of entrepreneurs. Such people can be found in any group of humans, but they do indeed have to be found, and they have to be given a chance.
- Finally, initial conditions need to be set in place so that IBM's original problem is avoided: radical ideas are allowed to grow instead of dying.

Incremental innovation was the subject of the previous chapter, so we will limit the discussion here to the other two foundations of radical innovation: entrepreneurship and initial conditions.

The entrepreneur is the one who "upsets and disorganizes," as discussed by Peter Drucker. The entrepreneur creates new, high-performing business systems through innovation and creative destruction. The entrepreneur assembles the required elements to exploit new opportunities: capital, people, innovative ideas, consumer needs, business models.

This requires the **radical thinking** that produces invention, new goals, and new means. To many people in business, the thought of "radical" ideas may be unnerving. Often radical is interpreted in the context of political action. There it means rebellion, with the aim to overthrow the government. There have been many examples where this leads to a future far worse than the past being replaced.

In the business context, the economist Joseph Schumpeter described capitalism as "creative destruction." Radical comes from the Latin "radix," meaning root. In philosophy, René Descartes compared radical thinking to the building of a house on solid foundations. The *Webster Collegiate Dictionary* defines radical as "of or relating to the origin; fundamental; marked by a considerable departure from the usual or traditional; extreme."

The radical thinker is fundamentally different from the incremental thinker, because he asks different questions:

Incremental thinking	Radical thinking
What is the current situation?	What is the current situation?
How much better could it be?	Where else could we go? Where do we want to go? What is the *opportunity*?
What do we need to do?	How do we get there?

The radical thinker is looking for significant changes to the current situation in terms of customer expectations, competitive advantage, and changing the game.

Favorable practices that foster radical innovation involve ideas and practices such as the following:

- Analyze life cycle. All businesses and business components have a short life expectancy. ("Where are we on the curve?")

- Analyze gap. Probable trend under current conditions vs. requisite, overarching target.
- Commit to systematic abandonment. Create space, free up resources. Abandon whatever is outworn, obsolete, no longer productive, as well as truthful analysis of mistakes, failures, and misdirection of effort in the past (e.g., three-year review: "Would we go into the business today?") Formulate an Entrepreneurial plan with objectives for innovation and deadlines. Allocate adequate resources.
- Set very high goals. Targets that cannot be achieved by extrapolating from the current business. Create a cause that will foster courage and devotion.
- Create a special focus on new ventures. It should be very high up. It will not happen without senior management leadership.
- Make people and units clearly accountable for innovation performance. There should be a systematic, disciplined process: manage by milestones, use prototyping.
- Organize the entrepreneurial, the new, separately from the old and the already existing. Do this perhaps totally, but certainly at least partially ("somewhat in, somewhat out").
- Account for new innovative efforts separately so that they do not have to carry burdens that they cannot yet bear.
- Use assets and competencies to define scenarios that are outside or redefine the current business domain.
- Bring new voices to the discussion, either internal or external; actually, both are necessary.
- Provide resources to create an open market for ideas, capital, and talents.
- Make many small bets early; avoid "bet the company" or "catch up to the first movers" big bets.
- Measure innovation performance specifically: built-in feedback within each project, portfolio analysis of all innovation projects.
- Pay innovative entrepreneurs well, very well.

Your corporate entrepreneurs are already inside your organization. Almost anyone who can face up to decision-making can learn to be an entrepreneur. Entrepreneurship is a behavior rather than a personality trait. It is based on a process rather than intuition.

Entrepreneurs are the drivers in the creation of the corporation's future. Developing entrepreneurs is one of the CEO's most critical tasks.

The CEO needs to spend a significant portion of his time on people development, career management, and personal presence at training programs. Only the CEO can set the high standards and support the behaviors that will change a company's current code.

One final point on **failure**: as long as they are not failures of character, failures are the key ingredient in learning and growth. Failure builds humility (but please don't repeat it). Film director William Ball provides the following wisdom:

> The greatest fear that an actor has is that he will fail in the part. All actors have that fear. At the beginning of the rehearsal process, I usually ask the assembled company, "Please think of the greatest successes you have had in your life and then think of the greatest failures. Which did you learn the most from, the failures or the successes?" Invariably, everyone has learned more from the failures. It is important to the creative process to recognize that we learn from our failures—much more than from our successes. Failure is the threshold of knowledge. Since new knowledge is that by which we progress, failure must be our constant companion. Every time we go through the doorway of knowledge, it is because we have stepped across a failure. We congratulate ourselves for failing. We fail boldly. We surround each other with love and enthusiasm after failure because we know that the failure took courage. On the other side of every failure is wisdom. Wisdom is growth, growth is progress, and progress is light. Failure is an integral part of life. Failure is a necessary and important part of the creative process. A director must encourage it and reward it, and he must tell actors

in advance that he values their failures. Otherwise, the actor learns to live in fear of failure. If he fears failure, his creativity is seriously impaired and he will not grow. It is important to "Fail Big!"

6.8   The IBM Example

The example of how IBM realized it had a problem at the level of game-changing new business initiatives and how it addressed it will provide a good base to propose a summary of useful guidelines on how to nurture radical innovation.

IBM recognized at a certain point that they were killing all their good ideas. They were surrendering new domain after new domain to startups or more aggressive established competitors. To add insult to injury, IBM had often been the inventor of what became a new, profitable market.

After much diagnostic and benchmarking, IBM concluded that new emerging businesses were being treated in the same way as older, established businesses within the corporation. This insured their death, since a baby is not an adult and cannot be expected to do the same things. In its benchmarking, IBM came upon a framework to improve its management of these different situations, each with a different "horizon," as follows:

- **Mature, well-established businesses** (H-1) provide more and better of the same. They are run by operators who apply strong discipline and a "no excuses" management style.
- **Rapidly growing businesses** (H-2) produce up to triple-digit growth. They are managed by business-building entrepreneurs looking to build personal wealth and to leave a legacy.
- **Emerging businesses** (H-3) are the subject of radical innovation. They are long term, most will not succeed, they require exploration skills. They are the domain of visionaries, unconventional thinkers who will champion them. Here it is the success rate that counts and progress is measured by project-based milestones.

For IBM, this framework, along with the allocation of sufficient resources and the appointment of leaders well respected throughout the organization, created a completely new set of winning conditions for emerging businesses. The details of this approach are documented in the Harvard Business case by Garvin and Levesque, referenced in the bibliography.

Chapter 7: Making It Happen

7.1   So ... Do We Have a Strategic Plan?

A recent workshop for Montreal members of the Institute of Corporate Directors provided a good opportunity to test the ideas in this book. Thirty corporate directors addressed the question, "How do we judge that this plan is a valid strategic plan?"

After reviewing the conceptual framework from this book, we all pressed on to the bottom line question: Do we have a valid strategy here? The group came up with four different and complementary approaches to answer the question.

I.   Is there an effective planning process?
- to achieve challenging goals?

II. Is there a factual assessment?
- What is the company's position on the life cycle curve and have its implications been clearly thought through?
- What happens if we maintain the status quo? The baseline forecast.

III. Is there an insightful strategy?
- Is the "opportunity" clearly identified?
- Will this strategy create a successful future for the company?
- Is this truly strategic or actually operational?
- Is there a clear and challenging vision, goal, target state?
- What is the value-creation proposition, the differentiation?
- Is this a compelling story? Is there buy-in from the team?
- Is this plan credible? Is it pragmatic? Does the company

have the experience, the positioning and the resources?
If not, how do we close the gap?

- Is there a Plan B?
- What are the costs, benefits, risks?
- How will we know we have been successful? What are the success criteria?

IV. Will there be disciplined follow-up?

- Is there a timeline?
- Execution: approach, program, follow-up?

You are halfway there once you are satisfied that there is indeed a valid strategic plan. What you have at that point is a plan. No action yet.

In order to transform plans into action, it is necessary to develop an approach to managing change, to choose a balanced sequence of moves, mostly in the form of projects, and disciplined follow-up. This is the subject of the next sections.

7.2   Managing Change

There is no generally accepted theory of managing change and changing minds. Yet business leaders have to manage change constantly and these waves of change are getting ever closer and ever bigger. A reasoned approach to each specific situation of change will increase the chances of acceptance, commitment, and successful implementation.

We will propose four ways to think about your change challenge and to formulate a plan for your specific situation.

I.   Changing Minds

The first condition of successful change is to change minds. This can be a long and difficult process, but it is mandatory, so it is better to start there first. Howard Gardner provides a useful framework.

The mind works through mental representations, ideas, concepts, stories, theories, and skills. Mental representations are **not** immutable; analysts of reflective individuals are able to lay them out, and, while altering representations may not be easy, changes can be affected. Moreover, because we have at our disposal so many mental representations that can be combined in so many ways, the possibilities are essentially limitless.

I argue here that multiple versions of the same point constitute an extremely powerful way in which to change minds. I have identified seven factors—sometimes I'll call them levers—that could be at work in all cases of a change of mind. As it happens each factor conveniently begins with the letter "re".

"Reason"; a rational approach, logic, analogies and making an overall assessment. **Research** of data or relevant cases leading to a judgment about whether a change of mind is warranted. **Resonance**; the extent to which a view, idea or perspective feels right to the individual, seems to fit the current situation. **Redescriptions**; a change of mind becomes convincing to the extent to it lends itself to representation in a number of different forms. **Resources and rewards** make mind change more likely to occur when considerable resources can be drawn upon. **Real world events** create conditions that support or impede a desired mind change (prosperity, war…). **Resistances** include acquired mind sets, the effort required to change. It is never easy to change minds. However, leaders of a relatively uniform group (such as a company) can present a story of somewhat greater complexity—perhaps even a "theory" of operations—than can the leader of a nation or one who leads across national boundaries.

In all cases, the same work must be done; analyse the current situation, determine what needs to change and envision an altered state of affairs. But for business leaders their audience is smaller, there is a common definition; they participate voluntarily, and temporarily. They likely have a common knowledge core, a common purpose, perhaps even a common destiny (if the corporation fails).[6]

II. The Nature of the Required Change

Change requires its own specific plan, in the same way that strategy requires a plan. It is necessary to define the target state, to figure out the type of change involved as well as the kind of environment where it will take place, the history, the levers and the barriers, the proposed approach, and an aligned action plan.

Except for entrepreneurs who thrive on it, most people find change difficult. They master the current system. Change will result in the reallocation of responsibilities and resources, and some may feel that they do not have the skills to succeed in the new environment.

The first step in defining an approach to change is understanding the drivers, the specific themes driving the change to be effected:

- Change in the mission or "raison d'être"?
- Change in identity or outside image?
- Change in relationships with key stakeholders?
- Change in the way of working?
- Change in the culture?

These drivers of change require qualification. Are they limited to specific areas of the company, or are they global? Do these changes require improvement or transformation? Can the issues of change be resolved through top-down authority, or do they require the whole enterprise system to participate in their resolution? **Incremental changes** that deal with structure and processes, what David Nadler calls "tuning" and "adaptation," are relatively simple. They require a sequential "first-things-first" approach. For example, a company

---

[6]   Howard Gardner, *Changing Minds* (Boston: Harvard Business School Press, 2004), pages 15, 16, 17 & 46.

creates an outcome by selling non-core assets or implements an improvement, such as finding new ways to reduce waste (lean manufacturing), which can be implemented within the current business model.

Discontinuous, **radical change** will result in a new business model. This is "reorientation" or "re-creation," again according to David Nadler. At this level of change, people need to adopt new behaviors, and the organization needs a new culture, for example, from reactive to proactive, from hierarchical to collegial, from introspective to extroverted. This obviously is the most complex type of alteration, and it certainly requires an approach quite different from those falling within the scope of incremental change.

III. Three Dimensions of Action

The third step is to make sure that all the levers that drive an organization are properly activated. These levers can be discussed in terms of **leadership, management,** and **politics**.

Leaders create the future. They have the clearest view of the goal, the vision. They also have the hardest, most clinical assessment of the current situation. They understand the gap and what is required to get from here to there: they create and manage the tension between the vision and the current situation.

Leaders are disruptive. In order to be effective, leaders need to have a broad, long-term perspective, a set of convictions about the company's direction, a clearly thought-out corporate philosophy, and an understanding of how to make the required changes happen.

In their book *The Leadership Engine*, Noël Tichy and Eli Cohen propose four dimensions of leadership that provide useful evaluation guides:

- **Ideas**: a clear idea of what it takes for the company or business unit to win and the capacity to constantly question and renew these ideas as reality changes.

- **Values:** clear and simple values that can be communicated and understood by all. The leader preaches by example in his daily actions.
- **Motivation:** high energy and the capacity to motivate others to high energy.
- **Edge:** the readiness to make hard decisions; the capacity to get others to do the same.

According to Bill George, retired CEO of Medtronic, the first and foremost leadership question is who you are. Leaders have followers. People follow leaders because they profit from it. This means economic profit, of course, but more importantly, personal growth. An authentic leader, according to George, works at this his whole life. In order to develop others, the leader's essential job, one has to develop oneself even further.

Planning change at the leadership level deals with finding the next big breakthrough, the next curve, helping people to buy in, and teaching by personal example.

Management tasks deal with performance. Superior managers create high performance. Performance can be measured in terms of time, money, tools, facilities, and physical resources. Management also deals with processes and functions, but most of all, managers help people to be the best that they can be at their job.

Performance of assets and processes calls on our rational, analytical skills. This is what we most often think of when we think of management. Any manager worth his salt must be good at that. But what distinguishes the great manager is discipline.

In a management context, discipline means consistently practiced regimens involving shared approaches to problems and decisions. Indeed, in order to successfully implement high-performance practices, businesses must first return to one of the oldest: the discipline of common methodologies and measures throughout the organization.

Planning change at the management level requires a review of policies and practices that specify daily activity. Is each one aligned to the target model, and if not, what is required?

In the context of business enterprise, **politics** is often perceived negatively. The fact that "politics are not tolerated here" is taken to be a mark of a strong, positive culture. In this context, politics means taking advantage of a situation for one's personal benefit or that of one's faction within the whole enterprise.

But when politics is considered as the function that exploits opportunities to achieve targeted results, then a very positive lever for implementing change emerges. The role of politics can be to negotiate and integrate divergent interests through creative compromise. The art of negotiation! Such positive political action contributes to accountability and democracy within the enterprise.

Broadly, the skills that enable political action are a realistic, pragmatic philosophy, a keen understanding of human nature, the capacity to build networks, and superior negotiating skills.

The skills of the politician are critical to successful change management because they are the skills required to deal with vested interests. Resources are always limited, and there will be competition among the various participants within the organization. This competition only increases when change creates more uncertainty. This is the domain of politics, which basically complements leadership vision and management processes.

In summary, leadership defines the vision, the target state; management develops and applies the protocols and processes that align daily activities to the vision; and politics creates the coalition that does it.

IV. Tactics

Finally, there is the question of tactics. It helps to look at radical change as a major project that surely will last over the medium term. It requires adequate resources. Here are some ideas:

- Create a "war room" where overall change and specific tactics will be planned, coordinated, measured, and evaluated.
- Gradually but inexorably shift leadership attention from those that oppose the change, the "anchor draggers," to those that are supporters, the early adopters, in order to create a **critical mass** for the new protocol.
- Give **middle management** frontline responsibility for the change. They understand the big picture, but they are also close enough to the action to actually transform daily activities.
- Create a lot of **projects** that are part of the new target state. Participants learn that they can win in the new order. Consequently, many new missionaries are created. A culture is not changed by working on the culture; it is changed by working on concrete projects.
- Provide **individual coaching** to help the members of the management team acquire the new mindset and behavior more rapidly and become more effective teachers.

The management literature is overfull with books and articles on managing change. The approach proposed by John Kotter in figure 7.1 is as good as any we have seen. It will provide you with a good starting point in planning the changes you wish to bring to your brownfield situation.

Kotter's process is top down driven change. It can be vastly enhanced if the phase dedicated to empowering others to act on the vision uses Henry Mintzberg's concept of organization as a community for its operating framework. Mintzberg argues that more progress will come from engaged management than heroic leadership.

Such engagement can be achieved through a process that builds from self-directed groups of middle managers meeting on their own time, say every two weeks over lunch for a period of 90 minutes. They are supplied with some orientation material, but essentially, managers learn as they discuss and reflect on their experiences in light of the conceptual material, learning from one another and developing actions for the workplace. Managers do this with little or no outside support. It is essentially up to themselves. Some have called this learning 2.0 to distinguish it from traditional lecturer driven training: **learning, not training**! These ideas are explained in Henry Mintzberg's recent book *Managing* and can be implemented with the help of his CoachingOurselves™ methodology .

Figure 7.1. Eight steps to transforming your organization.
Source: John P. Kotter, "Leading Change: Why Transforming Efforts Fail," *Harvard Business Review* March-April 1995.

7.3 Without Follow-up, Nothing Happens

At this point, plans for strategy, organization, and change must turn into **action**. This transition from planning to action involves its own set of possible problems:

- For some companies, strategic decisions are simply never executed.
- Others try to do everything at once: they overload the system, and gridlock is created. Much activity, few results.
- Others define a feasible program, but the portfolio of opportunities is not well balanced between "urgent" and "important" growth, innovation, and performance.
- No one is in charge of anything, and the plan becomes a memory.

There are guidelines and methodologies that can significantly increase the chances of successful implementation. Here are the guidelines we have found effective through time.

- **Projects create the difference:** The same system will produce the same results, whatever the budgets may indicate. It is well-chosen and well-executed projects that gradually strengthen and transform a business system to create a unique competitive edge. They should achieve high-impact results in a short time, they are staffed with people from different departments, they allow participants to experiment, and they adopt new directions and new cultures concretely.
- **Three to five projects at a time:** Significant accumulated experience in the field of continuous improvement (Hoshin planning) bears out the common-sense wisdom that pursuing too many targets at the same time leads to succeeding at none. Having three to five concurrent corporate initiatives appears to be the sweet spot for maximum performance. This is validated by another test. If you agree that "one battle per general" and "one general per battle" is a reasonable principle, you will find that the resources in your organization, the "generals"

that can lead key initiatives, may not be so numerous after you have taken account of current operations.

- **Quarterly pace:** Studies of companies with high success rates of new product introductions discovered that they were not necessarily the fastest. They did, however, maintain a regular, steady pace with iron discipline—for example, through management forums every three, four, or six months.
- **Balance:** In financial investments, selecting the right asset mix is deemed to account for the major part of performance; in corporate development, it is the selection of the best mix and sequence of project initiatives that adds up to superior total performance.
- **2X safety margin:** Whatever the growth/profit target, total project impact should aim for 2X of the target. This is simple prudence; some projects will fail, and even the winners most often take some time, or more time than anticipated, to reach their full potential.

The following sections describe a number of management practices that will help to continuously upgrade, learn, and follow up on the company's strategic development:

- Strategic initiatives: the President's Agenda
- Disciplined follow-up: the Management Forum
- A-B-C manpower inventory

This is not a complete set of practices, but they are a good start, and they are a demanding start.

7.4   Strategic Initiatives: The President's Agenda

The president's agenda provides sequence and balance to guide the execution of the strategic initiatives that give concrete expression to the strategic plan. Typically, strategic initiatives take the form of a project. Such projects should be structured to match the pace adopted by the company: three-, four-, or six-month cycles. Longer projects should have milestones to meet the chosen pace. In this way, all project leaders can report on project status at the management forum.

This allows the president to use the agenda as a fundamental tool for driving the organization forward:

- The agenda is aligned to the goals and the values pursued by the company.
- The agenda is balanced between strategic priorities, innovation, organization, and performance development priorities.
- The assignment and leadership for project outcomes is clear. Again "one general per battle, one battle per general."
- The agenda is widely communicated and people understand that the agenda is the way that strategy is being implemented.
- The agenda is integrated into the reward system.

A format to start developing your own agenda is illustrated in figure 7.2.

Illustrative initiatives	Q1	Q2	Q3	Q4
Strategic growth 1				
Strategic growth 2				
Innovation				
Performance				

Management forum   Management forum   Management forum   Management forum

Figure 7.2. The president's agenda—quarterly pace.

7.5 Disciplined Follow-up: The Management Forum

Leaders of high-performance organizations need a common space where they can define and follow up on the company's strategic initiatives. This workshop is not aimed at monitoring and correcting daily performance. Depending on their business, companies can accomplish that easily on a daily, weekly, or monthly basis. The management forum should take place one, two, three, or four times per year. It deals with the project initiatives in which consists the concrete implementation of the company's strategy.

The purpose of the management forum is to continuously update the company's goal and vision, to articulate it ever more clearly, and to relentlessly drive it to completion through follow-up and input on all critical strategic initiatives. The typical format is as follows:

- One- or two-day meeting on strategic priorities, held according to the pace required by the challenges at hand (e.g., quarterly).
- Participants:
    - Executive management
    - Key support staff
    - Guests (experts, clients, testimony from successful performance project teams)
- Methodology:
    - Individual presentations: results to date, gaps, next steps
    - Group discussion, constructive critique and contribution to each others' projects
    - Written and anonymous evaluation of individual presentations, as well as of overall progress toward company's strategic vision
- Required behavior:
    - Each manager develops and commits to a plan of action
    - Discussions are factual
    - Support and respect for others (e.g., company first, no personal accusations)
- Key success factors:
    - Decisions are made on the spot and individuals are committed to these decisions.
    - Individuals are accountable for achievement of project targets.
    - Individuals are responsible for demanding help as required
    - Colleagues provide support as required.

At the outset, success depends on making sure that each participant is well prepared before and after the meeting so that they clearly understand where they are coming from and integrating their concerns and challenges into projects that are aligned with the strategic intent. Here is how Jack Welch discussed his approach for the GE Corporate Executive Council:

> I operate on a simple belief about business. If there are six of us in a room, and we all get the same facts, in most cases, the six of us will reach roughly the same conclusion. And once we all accept that conclusion, we can force our energy into it and put it into action. The problem is, we don't get the same information. We each get different pieces. Business isn't complicated. The complications arise when people are cut off from information they need.[7]

7.6   A-B-C Management Inventory

"At the end of the day, you bet on people, not on strategies." This is how Larry Bossidy, then CEO of Allied Signal, made the point that organization, and particularly leadership, is the ultimate competitive advantage.

The foundation of building a championship management team is the A-B-C inventory of current management resources.

"A-B-C" refers to three levels of resources: "As" already have demonstrated the desired results and the attitudes; "Bs" can be far away from the target, but they have the potential to get to "A" level; "Cs" do not have the potential. When this analysis is applied for the first time, there is often great discomfort or disappointment, because most often, people realize that much effort and resource has been invested in the "Cs," who offer no potential for return. In our model companies, G.E. in this instance, leaders are categorized into four types:

- **Type I:** not only delivers on performance commitments, but believes in and furthers G.E.'s small-company values. ("small-company values" refers to G.E.'s definition of

---

[7]   Steven Kerr, "Speed, Simplicity, Self-Confidence: An Interview with Jack Welch," in *Ultimate Rewards* (Boston: Harvard Business Review, 1997).

entrepreneurship: simplicity, speed, and self-confidence).
For these people, onwards and upwards.

- **Type II:** does not meet commitments or share G.E.'s values—will not last long at G.E.
- **Type III:** believes in values but sometimes misses commitments. G.E. encourages taking risks, and type III is normally given another chance.
- **Type IV:** delivers short-term results, but without regard for values, by grinding people down, squeezing them, and stiffing them. Some of these individuals have learned to change; most couldn't. The decision to begin removing type IVs was a watershed, the ultimate test of G.E.'s ability to "walk the talk."

The ability to create a realistic and fair A-B-C inventory resides in having a transparent system of individual performance assessment. Typically, the big downfall here is discipline; 75 percent conformity just will not do. This is a moment of truth for a company's real leadership capacity and real commitment to be world class.

More specifically, the conditions required to make this process effective are as follows:

- Clear, mutual understanding of values and target performance results
- Sound leadership training
- Open discussion about what constitutes high performance
- Ethical, honest assessment process
- No vested interests
- Respect for the "Cs"

A wag once said, "Management is very tough work; that is why so very few people *do* it!"

The A-B-C inventory can be seen as the integration point in a process that builds a championship management team as illustrated in figure 7.3. Clear enterprise criteria provide the framework to assess individual skills and values, to identify gaps, and to format a development plan. Assessment of progress against the plan provides the input into the A-B-C inventory. Results from looking at the total pool of resources against company goals leads to group development initiatives. Then the cycle starts again.

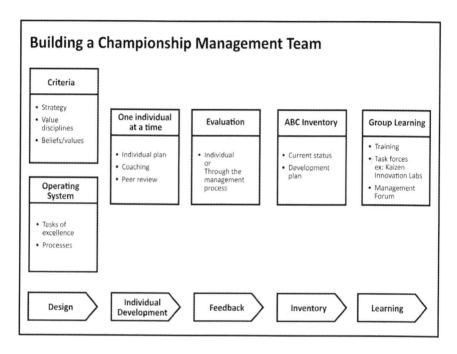

Figure 7.3. Building a championship management team.

7.7   Beware!

This journey starts with a decision to become a high performer capable of winning today and creating the future.

For greenfield situations, the problem is relatively simple: it is a question of going from the target state to execution. But even here, daily life will be at a demanding level; there will always be the temptation to water down or to adopt policies and practices that work against your organization's high-performance culture.

For brownfield situations, most often the greatest challenge will be implementing fundamental change. **Resistance** can come from unexpected sources.

1. **Management**. They have achieved their positions within the traditional hierarchy and culture. This is where they have been successful. Here, studies of revolutions are pertinent. Faced with a fundamental change, typically one third of the audience will be immediately supportive, one third will be strongly opposed to it, and the last third will go with the winners. Preparing these three lists is important; you don't want an opponent to be put in charge of a critical activity unless you think that you can turn him. Managing the list is critical. A company is not a parliament: there is neither the time nor the resources for endless debate. Here, "you are either with us or against us" is actually applicable.

2. **Corporate structure**. It contains many people who earn their living by mentoring and monitoring functions and programs over and into the operating units. Changing operating units to a high-performance model is a direct threat to the survival of many of them. It is to be expected that support will not be forthcoming from these areas.

3. **Accountant mindset**. Accountants bring value when they have a good business mindset. But sometimes they don't. They focus on "expense" instead of return on investment. As Ken Iverson of Nucor pointed out, your company may pay the highest individual salaries. Accountants will want to benchmark this and bring it into line. But this does not matter if your total labor cost is half the industry average, as is the case at Nucor. Accountants bring value, but in designing a business model, it's the business mind in them that we want.

4. **Human resources mindset**. Too many of human resources staff have been trained to manage a union contract. They are prisoners in that box: "What will the union think?" Well, most unions, like most people, prefer to be part of a high-performance environment—those who do not can learn to. Many other aspects of the traditional human resources doctrine go against some or many of the ideas presented in this book. So ask your human resources staff what their model is?

Last, but not least, someday you will be at the level of world-class performance. You will become, for that moment, **the establishment**. As Richard Pasquale pointed out, "Nothing fails like success." People of integrity, intelligence, and high commitment will tend to work very hard at repeating a successful formula. They are winning today but failing to create the future. A part of your and your company's brain must start every day from scratch.

7.8   A Journey to Mastery

Achieving world-class performance—winning today and being able to create the future—is first of all an act of leadership.

As Edwards W. Deming put it, "The job of management is not supervision, but leadership. Leaders must know the work that they supervise. Managers must work on sources of improvement, the intent of quality of product and service, and on the translation of the intent into design and actual product." When managers develop systems fostering high commitment, workers do high performance work.

This requires a decision to get out of your comfort zone, to be humble in order to be able to learn new things. It is a journey that lasts forever.

In a business context, the CEO plays a critical role because he sets the bar high and creates or acts to support the creation of conditions for high performance to be achieved. But actually, this requires the commitment of everyone in the organization; the chain is as strong as its weakness link. Each person in the organization needs to become a master at his job.

In his book *Mastery*, George Leonard discusses the nature of mastery as follows:

> It resists definition yet can be instantly recognized. It comes in many varieties, yet follows certain unchanging laws. It brings rich rewards, yet is not really a goal or a destination but rather a process, a journey. We call this journey mastery, and tend to assume that it requires a special ticket available only to those born with exceptional abilities. But **mastery** isn't reserved for the supertalented or even for those who are fortunate enough to have gotten

an early start. It's available to anyone who is willing to get on the path and stay on it—regardless of age, sex, or previous experience.

The trouble is that we have few, if any, maps to guide us on the journey or even to show us how to find the path. The modern world, in fact, can be viewed as a prodigious conspiracy against mastery. We're continually bombarded with promises of immediate gratification, instant success, and fast, temporary relief, all of which lead in exactly the wrong direction.

The journey to mastery requires commitment and consistency. Not all who try stay on the path. Leonard identifies four different types of people who start on the journey, and those that actually achieve mastery. Figure 7.4 presents these different types.

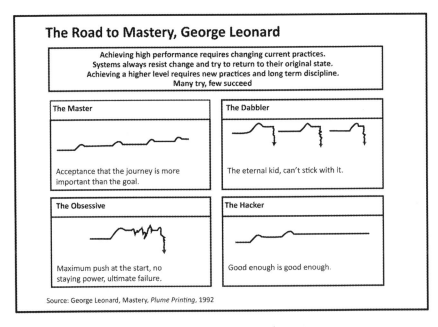

Figure 7.4. The road to mastery—George Leonard.
Source: George Leonard, *Mastery* (New York: Plume Printing, 1992).

So what is it that differentiates the master, what Bill George calls the **authentic leader**?

> I believe that leadership begins and ends with authenticity. It's being yourself; being the person you were created to be. This is not what most of the literature on leadership says, nor is it what the experts in corporate America teach. Instead, they develop lists of leadership characteristics one is supposed to emulate. They describe the styles of leaders and suggest that you adopt them.
>
> Authentic leaders genuinely desire to serve others through their leadership. They are more interested in empowering the people they lead to make a difference than they are in power, money, or prestige for themselves. They are as guided by qualities of the heart, by passion and compassion, as they are by qualities of the mind.
>
> Authentic leaders are not born that way. Many people have natural leadership gifts, but they have to develop them fully to become outstanding leaders. Authentic leaders use their natural abilities, but they also recognize their shortcomings and work hard to overcome them. They lead with purpose, meaning, and values. They build enduring relationships with people. Others follow them because they know where they stand. They are consistent and self-disciplined. When their principles are tested, they refuse to compromise. Authentic leaders are dedicated to developing themselves because they know that becoming a leader takes a lifetime of personal growth.[8]

So, is all this possible? You know the answer to that: everything is possible.

---

[8] Bill George, *Authentic Leadership* (Toronto: John Wiley & Sons, 2004), pages 11-12.

Bibliography

Alinsky, S. D. *Rules for Radicals: A Pragmatic Primer for Realistic Radicals*. New York: Random House.

Ball, William. *A Sense of Direction.* Hollywood, California: Quite Specific Media Group Ltd., 1984.

Baron, James N. and David M. Kreps. *Strategic Human Resources.* New York: John Wiley & Sons Inc., 1999.

Bonaparte, Napoleon, *Comment faire la guerre*, Éditions Champ Libre, Paris, 1973.

Bossidy, Larry, and Ram Charan. *Execution.* New York: Crown Business, 2002.

Charan, Ram, and Noel M. Tichy. *Every Business Is a Growth Business.* New York: Time Business, 1998.

Christensen, Clayton M. *The Innovator's Dilemma.* Boston: Harvard Business School Press, 1997.

Cooper, Robert G. *Winning at New Products.* Gage, 1987.

Collins, Jim. *Good to Great.* New York: Harper Business, 2001.

Deming, Edward D. *Out of the Crisis.* Boston: Massachusetts Institute of Technology, 1982.

Drucker, Peter F. *Innovation and entrepreneurship*, New York: Harper & Row, 1985.

———. *Theory of the Firm,* Boston: Harvard Business Review, 1998.

The Economist. "Might the Proper Study of Management Be Man?" April 17, 2004.

The Financial Times. *Handbook of Management.* London: Pitman Publishing, 1995.

Foster, Richard N. *Innovation, the Attackers' Advantage.* New York: Summit, 1986.

Foster, Richard, and Sarah Kaplan. *Creative Destruction.* New York: Currency Doubleday, 2001.

Franklin, Carl. *Why Innovation Fails.* London: Spiro Press, 2003.

Gardner, Howard. *Changing Minds.* Boston: Harvard Business School Press, 2004.

Garvin, David A., and Lynne C. Levesque. *Emerging Business Opportunities at IBM A, B, C.* Boston: Harvard Business Review, 9-304-075, -076 and -077, February 28, 2005.

George, Bill. *Authentic Leadership.* San Francisco: Jossey-Bass, 2003.

Goldenberg, Jacob, Donald Leherman, and David Magursky. *Marketing Science Institute*, 1999.

Goold, Michael, and Andrew Campbell. "Do You Have a Well-Designed Organization?" Boston:, March 2002.

Hamel, Gary. *The Future of Management.* McGraw-Hill, 2007.

Hamel, Gary, and Prahalad, C. K. "Strategic Intent" Boston: Harvard Business Review, May-June 1989.

Huston, Larry, and Nabil Sakkab. "Connect and Develop" Boston: Harvard Business Review, March 2006.

IBM. *The Enterprise of the Future*, White Plains: IBM Global CEO Study, 2008.

Inverson, Ken. *Plain Talk.* New York: John Wiley & Sons, 1998 .

Jaques, Elliott. "In Praise of Hierarchy" Boston: Harvard Business Review, January-February 1990.

Kerr, Steven. "Speed, Simplicity, and Self-Confidence: An Interview with Jack Welch," *Ultimate Rewards*. Boston: Harvard Business Review Book, 1997.

Kiechel, Walter III, *The Lords of Strategy* Boston: Harvard Business Press, 2010.

Kim, W. Chan, and Renée Mauborgne. *Blue Ocean Strategy*. Boston: Harvard Business School Press, 2005.

Knight, Charles F. "Emerson Electric: Consistent Profits, Consistently" Boston: Harvard Business Review January-February 1992.

Kotler, Philip, and Ronald E. Turner. *Marketing Management* 6th and 7th ed. Englewood Cliffs, New Jersey: Prentice-Hall, 1989.

Kotter, John P. *"Leading Change: Why Transforming Efforts Fail"* Boston: Harvard Business Review, March-April 1995.

Laurie, Donald L., et al. "Creating New Growth Platforms" Boston: Harvard Business Review, May 2006.

Lawler, Edward E. *Treat People Right!* San Francisco: Jossey-Bass, 2003.

Lawler, Edward E., Susan Albers Mohrman, and Gerald E. Ledford. *Creating High Performance Organizations.* San Francisco: The Jossey-Bass Management Series, 1995.

Leonard, George. *Mastery.* New York: Plume, 1992.

Liker, Jeffrey K. *The Toyota Way.* New York: McGraw-Hill, 2004.

Luttwak, Edward N. *Strategy: The Logic of War and Peace.* Cambridge: The Belkrap Press, 1987.

Mintzberg, Henry. *America's Scorched Management.* Project Syndicate, July 29, 2008.

Mintzberg, Henry. *Managing.* San Francisco: Berrett-Koehler Publishers, 2009.

———. "The Fall and Rise of Strategic Planning" Boston: Harvard Business Review, January-February 1994.

Nadler, David A., Marc S. Gerstein, and Robert B. Shan. *Organizational Architecture.* San Francisco: Jossey-Bass, 1992.

Nonaka, Ikujiro, and Hirotaka Takeuchi. *The Knowledge Creating Company,* New York: Oxford University Press, 1995.

Ohmae, Kenichi. *The Mind of the Strategist.* New York: Penguin Books, 1982.

Ouimet, Gérard. *Le pouvoir politique du dirigeant d'entreprise: perversité ou nécessité?* Montréal, Gestion, printemps, 2005.

Pagonis, William G., and Jeffrey L. Cruikshank. *Moving Mountains: Lessons in Leadership and Logistics from the Gulf War.* Boston: Harvard Business School Press, 1992.

Pascale Tanner, Richard. *Managing on the Edge.* New York: Simon and Schuster, 1990.

Popper, Karl. *The Myth of the Framework.* London: Routledge, 1994.

———. *Unended Quest.* London: Routledge, 1992.

Porter, Michael E. "What Is Strategy?" Boston: Harvard Business Review, November-December 1996.

Roberts, John. *The Modern Firm.* New York: Oxford University Press, 2004.

Shaffer, Robert H. "Demand Better Results and Get Them" Boston: Harvard Business Review, March-April 1991.

Sharma, Anand, and Patricia E. Moody. *The Perfect Engine*. New York: The Free Press, 2001.

Stalk, George, and Rob Lachenauer. *Hardball*. Boston: Harvard Business School Press, 2004.

Thain, Donald H. "Managing the Strategic Agenda: The CEO's Job 1," *Business Quarterly*, March 22, 2003. London, Ontario: The University of Western Ontario.

Tichy, Noël M., and Stratford Sherman. *Control Your Destiny or Someone Else Will*. New York: Doubleday, 1993.

Tichy, Noël M., with Eli Cohen. *The Leadership Engine*. New York: Harper Business, 1997.

Womack, James P., and Daniel T. Jones. *Lean Thinking*. New York: Simon & Schuster, 1996.

About the Author

Michel David has worked in strategy and leadership for the past thirty-five years. His clients have included companies that are world leaders as well as emerging small and medium enterprises. He has been a senior partner with one of the world's leading consulting firms, and for the past twenty years he has operated a boutique consultancy based in Montreal.

Throughout his career, the consulting approach has been to involve clients deeply in the process so that it actually becomes *their* process. This mass of experience has provided the know-how required to propose an effective process for companies to design and execute successful strategies to create a winning future

Michel lives in Montreal, Canada. He is an associate of Henry Mintzberg's CoachingOurselves Network and a member of the Program Committee of the Ecole d'Entrepreneurship de Beauce. In December 2007, he received his black belt in Kyokushin karate.

Acknowledgments

The following people had the patience to put up with the many drafts of this book. They were kind enough to provide positive criticism and insight at times when this project did not really look viable.

- Francine Belzile
- Edith Bienvenue
- Herb Brown
- Angela Burlton
- Mao Hua Chen
- Yvon Chouinard
- Bernard Colas
- Daniel Cohen
- John Curtis
- Yvon D'Anjou
- Jerome Davis
- Michel de Grandpré
- Marc Dutil
- Luc Lajoie
- Hélène Laplante
- Olivier Laquinte
- Michel Lozeau
- Michel Marcoux
- Marc Mellinger
- Marcel Pinchevsky
- Huguette Noël
- Johanne Queenton
- Michel Peterson
- Jean Phaneuf
- Robert Potvin
- Pierre Robitaille
- Anand Sharma
- Philippe Telio
- Kristina Tomaz-Young
- Robert Turgeon